HOW TO COOK A STEAK

(and Other Life-Changing Recipes to Elevate the Food You Already Cook)

MIKE ALFARAH
Creator of Alf's Kitchen

PAGE STREET
PUBLISHING CO.

First published in 2024 by

Page Street Publishing Co.

27 Congress Street, Suite 1511

Salem, MA 01970

www.pagestreetpublishing.com

Distributed by Macmillan, sales in Canada by The Canadian Manda Group.

28 27 26 25 24   1 2 3 4 5

ISBN-13: 979-88900-3037-5

Library of Congress Control Number: 2023944957

Edits by Marissa Giambelluca

Cover and book design by Molly Kate Young for Page Street Publishing Co.

Photography by Corey Wyckoff

Printed and bound in China

DEDICATION

This book is dedicated to all of my incredible family and friends who have been such a huge support on this crazy journey. A very big thank you to my girlfriend, Amber, and son, Bryson, for always cheering me on during the countless hours of preparation and work on this book. Amber, you were amazing throughout this process with all your help in making sure I had the time and space to work on everything behind the scenes. As more doors open, life gets more hectic, but you both make everything worth it.

Creating this book took a lot of patience, time, and hard work . . . and without you, it would not have been possible. Thank you for everything, and I love you both very much.

CONTENTS

INTRODUCTION

Cooking for family and friends has been at the center of my life for as long as I can remember. If you are reading this book, you are about to uncover my tried-and-true recipes that bring you the best version of so many of your favorite dishes. I'm a firm believer in breaking down barriers in the culinary world. We all should respect traditions and the traditional approach to staple dishes from across the world, but never let tradition get in the way of innovation. Whether you are new to cooking or a seasoned chef, my goal is to help shed some light on the ways you can use different flavors to elevate some of your favorite meals.

This book is rooted in my passion for sharing what I've learned in over twenty years of "cooking outside the box." I'm not a traditionally trained chef by any means, but I've learned through doing just like so many of you have. Let's face it, it's hard to find a better feeling than the one you get when you see family and friends enjoy the food you created and poured your heart into. Throughout this book, you'll find unique flavor combinations as well as techniques that will help you leave a lasting impression in the kitchen. Not only will these recipes impress those around you, but they will also breathe new life into some of those classic dishes we all know and love.

My culinary journey has been a long one, and getting to this point was only possible by keeping an open mind and not being afraid to try something new. I first found my love for cooking at a young age. I remember finally being old enough to help with some minor prep work around holidays and cookouts when I was over at my grandparents' house. It was so easy to fall in love with the idea of putting together all these simple ingredients to make something that my loved ones could enjoy. I mean who doesn't love food!? And since I was artistic by nature, it was a match made in heaven. My life has had its ups and downs, but no matter where I was in life, I could always find comfort in the kitchen.

I have an entire chapter of this book dedicated to pizza because my first job in the culinary space was at a local pizza shop. My favorite part of that job was working with friends and having these fun competitions in who could make the best pizza of the night. I would often run to the store and grab crazy ingredients to bring to work the next day to really blow everyone away. At this stage I was obsessed with trying to understand what flavors work well with each other, and this obsession was only made worse by watching one of my favorite shows, *Chopped*. I would challenge myself by doing my own version of this show at home, and I loved every minute of it.

When the world came to a screeching halt with the pandemic in 2020, I created a TikTok account to start sharing more of my recipes. My first video got over 1,000 views without any followers, and I was hooked. To say I was motivated to keep creating would be a massive understatement. I started posting my favorite recipes under the name Alf's Kitchen, with step-by-step instructions on how to make each recipe, and before I knew it, I found myself immersed in an amazing community that loved sharing unique recipes as much as I do.

It's safe to say that using social media to share my recipes reignited my passion for experimenting in the kitchen as well as pushing boundaries as a home cook. This really resonated with people as my audience grew, because my approach to the recipes that I share is to always make others feel like they can make it along with me. Entertainment and education are always at the center of what I create.

Fast forward to today and my community has grown to be one of the most engaged and open-minded ones on social media. I love connecting with all of you as well as helping those who reach out with questions about improving in the kitchen. I am humbled daily by the people who share ideas, leave feedback, and show support on this crazy journey. The community we are building online is amazing, and now I get to welcome so many more of you into it with this book. My mission is to make great food more accessible. You don't need fancy equipment, years of training, or a lot of money to make amazing food to share with those you love. I am so excited to bring some of my favorite recipes right to you and even more excited to see your recreations online. This book is going to help you find comfort and excitement in letting new flavors shine in classic dishes.

ELEVATED ENTRÉES

The star of the show at every meal is the main course, and that's why we are starting the book off here. Get ready to find some favorite dishes while also falling in love with new flavor combinations served up in a familiar way. I am so excited to kick things off with the dish I've built my reputation on, a perfect The Perfect Steak (page 11). The reverse sear method is my go-to for a perfect edge-to-edge cook and a sear that can't be beat. The slow and controlled cook using this method makes preparing an incredible steak far less intimidating. I also get to show you My Signature Smash Burger (page 15), which really demonstrates how something can be simple at its core but packed with flavor in every bite. A smash burger gives you a very flavorful and caramelized crust, while also taking all the guesswork out of trying to get it to a medium or medium-rare temperature. By the time you are finished with this chapter, you will have an entirely new outlook on what makes the perfect entrée.

THE PERFECT STEAK

Yield: 2–3 servings

Steak with compound butter is the one meal I am asked to make more than anything else. Even my son, Bryson, has been obsessed with steak since before he was two years old. I love cooking steak, whether it's over charcoal, in a skillet, sous vide or on the smoker . . . but my favorite way is any version using the reverse sear method. The result is always a perfect edge-to-edge cook and a juicy steak that is elevated by an incredibly flavorful finishing butter called Café de Paris butter. The butter has a lot of ingredients, and they all play a key role in the flavor development. So when you pair this up with a steak, you have a guaranteed winner every time.

For the Steak

2 bone-in ribeye steaks, 1–1½ inches (2.5–4 cm) thick

1 tsp coarse kosher salt

1 tsp ground black pepper

For the Café de Paris Butter

½ cup (113 g) softened butter

2 tbsp (20 g) diced shallots

2 cloves garlic, minced

3 anchovy fillets, diced (or substitute ¾ tsp anchovy paste)

1 tsp lemon juice

1 tsp Worcestershire sauce

1 tsp Dijon mustard

1 tsp mild curry powder

½ tsp paprika

2 tsp (4 g) fresh finely chopped tarragon

2 tsp (4 g) fresh finely chopped parsley

2 tbsp (30 ml) avocado oil

Preheat your smoker or oven to 225°F (107°C).

Season each steak generously with the salt and pepper. Place the steaks on a wire rack set over a baking sheet. This setup allows hot air to circulate around the steaks, which helps get an even cook. If using your smoker, place the steaks directly on the grates. The key to getting a perfectly cooked steak comes from cooking to a specific internal temperature, not time. No steak is created equally, and they all reach your desired internal temperature at a different time. If you are aiming for medium-rare doneness, the first stage of cooking will take 45 to 60 minutes, or until the internal temperature reaches 120°F (49°C) when checked with a meat thermometer.

While the steaks are cooking, let's prepare the Café de Paris Butter. In a small bowl, combine the softened butter with the shallots, garlic, anchovies, lemon juice, Worcestershire sauce, Dijon mustard, curry powder, paprika, tarragon and parsley. Mix this well and make sure all the ingredients are evenly distributed. Set the butter aside to further develop flavor.

Once the steaks have reached the desired temperature for the first stage, take them out of the oven or smoker and let them rest for 3 to 5 minutes. While you wait, heat a stainless steel pan over high heat and add the avocado oil. Once the oil is shimmering and up to temperature, add the steaks and sear for 45 to 60 seconds per side. I also always recommend using a steak press to get the best surface contact, which will give you a perfect sear every time. Transfer the steaks to a cutting board and let them rest for 5 minutes. Cut the steaks against the grain and serve with a generous dollop of the Café de Paris Butter on top. It will melt over the steak, giving each bite an extra pop of flavor.

GRILLED HARISSA LAMB CHOPS WITH MINT CHIMICHURRI

Yield: 2–3 servings

When making the best version of lamb chops, I couldn't help but be inspired by Middle Eastern cuisine. This dish brings the heat from a North African chili paste known as harissa. To balance it out, I like to serve the chops with a refreshing South American chimichurri sauce. We grill the lamb chops to medium-rare perfection, resulting in tender and juicy meat that brings a delicious smoky flavor and pairs perfectly with the bold and refreshing flavors of the chimichurri.

For the Lamb Chops

2 tbsp (30 ml) avocado oil (if using stovetop)

2–3 lb (900 g–1.4 kg) lamb chops (6–8 individual chops)

Salt and pepper, as needed

¼ cup (60 ml) harissa paste

¼ cup (60 ml) olive oil

For the Mint Chimichurri

½ cup (8 g) fresh chopped cilantro

½ cup (8 g) fresh chopped mint

½ cup (8 g) fresh chopped flat-leaf parsley

3 cloves garlic, minced

¼ tsp crushed red chili flakes

2 tbsp (30 ml) red wine vinegar

1 tbsp (15 ml) lemon juice

½ cup (120 ml) extra virgin olive oil

Preheat your grill to high heat. Any grill will work for this, but for the best results, use charcoal or a wood fire. If you don't have a grill, you can use your stovetop and oven—just preheat the oven to 375°F (190°C). You will also need to grab an oven-safe skillet and heat the avocado oil over medium-high heat.

While the grill is coming up to temperature, prepare the lamb chops by seasoning all sides of each chop with salt and pepper. In a small bowl, mix together the harissa paste and olive oil. Brush the sauce on both sides of each lamb chop.

If cooking on a grill: I prefer a medium-rare doneness to maximize the flavor and juiciness of the meat, so I cook the chops for 3 to 4 minutes per side to achieve that. You can adjust the time for your preference; 5 to 6 minutes will lead to a more medium-well or well-done finish. Remove the lamb chops from the grill and let them rest for at least 5 minutes on a cutting board with a loose aluminum foil tent placed over the top of them.

If using an oven and stovetop, start by searing each side of the lamb chops for 1 to 2 minutes in the preheated skillet. Once you are happy with the sear, place the skillet directly in the oven to help them finish to your desired internal temperature. Start checking the internal temperature periodically with a meat thermometer after 3 to 5 minutes, and when the lamb chops reach 5 degrees under your desired doneness you can remove them from the oven and let them rest on a cutting board with a loose aluminum foil tent placed over the top.

While the lamb chops rest, make the mint chimichurri. Grab a food processor and add the cilantro, mint, parsley, garlic, red chili flakes, red wine vinegar and lemon juice. You are looking for a uniform mixture and the best way to achieve that is by processing on low for 15 to 20 seconds at a time until you reach the right consistency. Then, slowly add the olive oil to the food processor and pulse the mixture until it's smooth. By now, the lamb chops will be ready, and you can serve them up with a drizzle of mint chimichurri over the top and enjoy this incredible pairing of flavors.

MY SIGNATURE SMASH BURGER

Yield: 4 burgers

Simplicity isn't always a bad thing, especially when these ingredients carry so much flavor on their own. The caramelized onions add so much depth of flavor that complement the crispy beef patties so well. American cheese, love it or hate it, makes for the best cheese on a smash burger hands-down. And topping it off with my burger sauce takes it to an entirely new level. Feel free to dress it up with additional toppings or let the simple-yet-incredible flavors shine through on their own.

For the Caramelized Onions

2 tbsp (28 g) butter

1 tbsp (15 ml) olive oil

2 large onions, thinly sliced

1 tsp salt

½ tsp black pepper

For the Burgers

2 lb (900 g) ground beef (80-percent lean)

Salt and black pepper, as needed

8 slices of cheese (American, Cheddar, Pepper Jack or your favorite)

4 burger buns

For the Signature Burger Sauce

½ cup (120 ml) mayonnaise

¼ cup (60 ml) barbeque sauce of choice (preferably with pepper)

2 tbsp (30 ml) mustard

We're going to start by making our caramelized onions. In a large skillet, melt the butter with the olive oil over medium-low to medium heat. Add the onions and season them with salt and pepper. Let them cook in the oil and butter, stirring occasionally, for 40 to 45 minutes, or until they become caramelized and turn a golden brown. When they are ready, remove them from the heat and set aside.

For the burgers, preheat a cast-iron skillet or griddle over medium-high heat. Divide the ground beef into eight equal portions, 3 to 4 ounces (85 to 113 g) apiece, shaping each portion into a ball. Season one side of each beef ball with salt and pepper.

Place a beef ball onto the preheated skillet or griddle, seasoned side down. Using a burger press or spatula, press down, firmly flattening the ball into a patty that's as thin as you can get while holding still holding its circular shape. This is the key to getting the caramelized crispy edges that make a smash burger so good. Repeat with each beef ball. Season the top sides of the patties with a sprinkle of salt and pepper. Cook for 2 to 3 minutes, or until the edges turn brown and crispy. The burgers will cook 80 to 90 percent of the way on this first side.

Give the patties a flip and place a slice of your favorite cheese on top of each patty. Move the cooked burgers over to the cooler side of the griddle or to a sheet pan if using a skillet, to allow the cheese to finish melting and the burger to rest a moment. Give the buns a quick toast on the griddle or skillet as well and set them aside.

While the patties are resting, let's make my signature burger sauce. Combine the mayonnaise, barbecue sauce and mustard in a small bowl and mix well. It's a very simple sauce, but the flavor is on another level.

To build the best possible burger, start by adding ⅛ to ¼ cup (30 to 60 g) of caramelized onions to the bottom bun. Then place down two of the smash burger patties and spread a generous amount of my signature burger sauce on the top bun. Place the bun on top and you are ready to enjoy my favorite burger.

LAMB BURGER WITH TZATZIKI SAUCE

Yield: 4 lamb burgers

The first time I had a lamb burger was at this amazing food spot in downtown Toledo, Ohio, called Souk. It was a twist on kofta, and I made it a goal to find a way to make a lamb burger of my own that I could share with friends and family. I imagined a tender lamb patty seasoned with Mediterranean spices, topped with a refreshing tzatziki sauce and nestled between brioche buns . . . and I made it happen. This burger has the flavors I love from a traditional gyro but with a burger-style makeover that will blow your mind.

For the Tzatziki Sauce

½ cup (120 ml) Greek yogurt

¼ cup (60 g) grated cucumber

1 tbsp (15 ml) lemon juice

1 tbsp (4 g) chopped fresh dill

1 clove garlic, minced

Salt and black pepper, to taste

For the Lamb Burgers

1 lb (454 g) ground lamb

¼ cup (30 g) breadcrumbs

¼ cup (30 g) finely chopped red onion

2 cloves garlic, minced

1 tsp dried oregano

½ tsp ground cumin

Salt and black pepper, as needed

For Serving

4 brioche burger buns

Lettuce leaves

Sliced tomatoes

Sliced red onion

Let's start by making the tzatziki sauce. In a bowl, combine the yogurt, cucumber, lemon juice, dill, garlic, salt and pepper. One very important step is to remove some of the moisture from the grated cucumbers by placing them on a clean kitchen towel and squeezing them out. After making sure everything is mixed well, take a quick taste, and adjust the seasoning to your preference. Set the tzatziki in the fridge to develop flavor while you cook the burgers.

To make the burgers, grab a large mixing bowl and add the ground lamb, breadcrumbs, onion, garlic, oregano, ground cumin, salt and pepper. Mix thoroughly and divide the mixture into four equal portions before forming each into a patty.

Preheat your grill or skillet over medium-high heat. Once it's hot, place the lamb patties on the grill or skillet and cook for 4 to 5 minutes per side. Keep an eye on them and adjust the cooking time to achieve your desired level of doneness. Make sure to let the lamb burgers rest when done to get the best result.

Now it's time to assemble the burger. Take the bottom bun and spread a generous amount of the tangy tzatziki sauce. Place down lettuce leaves on top of the sauce, followed by sliced tomato, a lamb patty, more of the tzatziki sauce, and sliced red onion. These toppings pair perfectly with the flavors of the sauce and lamb. Finally, place the top bun on the burger, and you are ready to dive right in.

FRIED GREEN TOMATO PO' BOY

Yield: 4 po' boys

When I'm lucky enough to visit any of my family in the South, I get excited knowing I'll experience some incredible food with great company. Some of the most amazing meals I've had were on trips to Mississippi on the Gulf Coast. One of the biggest standouts of my latest trip was the fried green tomato po' boy I had when I was in New Orleans. When you think of a po' boy, fried green tomatoes are usually not the first thing that come to mind. It's no secret I love meat-based dishes, so when I tell you that this vegetarian po' boy puts any other version to shame, you know it's serious. This sandwich combines crispy fried green tomatoes with a zesty remoulade sauce alongside other fresh toppings. The French baguette pulls it all together and this sandwich is something else.

For the Fried Green Tomatoes

2 large green tomatoes

1 cup (120 g) all-purpose flour

1 tsp paprika

½ tsp salt

¼ tsp pepper

2 eggs, beaten

1 quart (1 L) vegetable oil, for frying

For the Remoulade

½ cup (120 ml) mayonnaise

2 tbsp (30 ml) Creole mustard (or substitute Dijon mustard)

1 tbsp (15 ml) hot sauce (adjust to taste)

1 tbsp (4 g) chopped fresh parsley

1 tbsp (4 g) chopped green onions

1 clove garlic, minced

Salt and black pepper, to taste

For Serving

4 soft French baguettes or hoagie rolls

Shredded lettuce

Julienned pickles

Julienned tomatoes

Julienned red onion

Slice the tomatoes into ¼-inch (6-mm)-thick rounds. Grab a shallow dish and combine the flour, paprika, salt and pepper to form the coating. Crack the eggs into a separate dish and beat them for 20 to 30 seconds. Dip each tomato slice into the beaten eggs, coating both sides. Then coat each tomato slice into the flour mixture. Make sure the coating is even, and shake off the excess flour.

Heat the oil in a large skillet over medium-high heat. Fry the tomato slices in batches for 2 to 3 minutes per side, or until they turn golden brown and crispy. Remove the tomatoes, and place them on a paper towel–lined plate to remove any excess oil.

To make the remoulade, in a small bowl, combine the mayonnaise, Creole mustard, hot sauce, parsley, green onions, garlic, salt and pepper. Give it a good stir, and feel free to adjust the seasoning to your preference.

Now we can build our sandwich. Slice the French baguettes lengthwise, but make sure not to cut all the way through. Spread a generous amount of the remoulade sauce on the bottom half of each baguette. Then place a layer of fried green tomatoes on top of the sauce. Top the tomatoes with the lettuce, pickles, tomatoes and red onion. I love these toppings because they add texture and balance to our sandwich. Serve your po' boys with your favorite side or potato chips, and get ready for a flavor bomb. This dish takes me back to eating fresh fried green tomatoes with my grandparents as a kid, and it's one I recommend to anyone who has never tried them.

PULLED PORK WITH PINEAPPLE SLAW

Yield: 8-10 servings

When I got my Traeger® grill, I was so excited to make pulled pork for the first time because of the vast differences in the wood smoke, seasoning and marinade options out there. This is my absolute favorite pulled pork recipe with a refreshing pineapple slaw; the hints of sweetness, acidity and bright flavors perfectly complement the smoky richness of our pulled pork. You will never catch me at a barbecue without this slaw if pulled pork is on the menu.

For the Pork

¼ cup (50 g) brown sugar

1 tbsp (8 g) paprika

1 tbsp (8 g) garlic powder

1 tbsp (8 g) onion powder

1 tbsp (8 g) chili powder

2 tbsp (30 g) salt

2 tbsp (16 g) black pepper

5-6 lb (2.3-2.7 kg) pork shoulder or pork butt

¼-½ cup (60-120 ml) yellow mustard

½ cup (120 ml) apple cider vinegar

½ cup (120 ml) apple juice

1-2 cups (240-480 ml) barbecue sauce

For the Slaw

2 cups (200 g) shredded cabbage

1 cup (165 g) diced pineapple

¼ cup (15 g) chopped fresh cilantro

¼ cup (60 ml) mayonnaise

1 tbsp (15 ml) apple cider vinegar

1 tbsp (15 ml) honey

Salt and black pepper, to taste

Soft hamburger buns, for serving

Fire your smoker up to 250°F (121°C) for a perfect low and slow cook. If you don't have a smoker, you can use the oven preheated to 250°F (121°C).

In a small bowl, combine the brown sugar, paprika, garlic powder, onion powder, chili powder, salt and pepper. Mix it well and set aside. Coat the outside of the pork shoulder with the yellow mustard. This will act as a binder for our seasoning, which helps it stick but doesn't affect the flavor of the pork. Generously rub the seasoning all over the pork shoulder and ensure all sides are covered. Then combine the apple cider vinegar and apple juice into a spray bottle and take that with you out to the smoker.

Place the seasoned pork shoulder in the pre-heated smoker. I like to place it on a cooling rack and place that directly on the grates. This helps make taking it off the smoker much easier. If you are using an oven, place the pork shoulder on a cooling rack on top of a baking sheet before placing it in the oven. Smoke or bake for 4 hours, spraying with the apple cider vinegar and apple juice mixture every 30 to 60 minutes.

After the first 4 hours, remove the pork shoulder and spray it down once more before you wrap the entire thing in peach butcher paper. Smoke or bake at 250°F (121°C) for 4 more hours, or until the internal temperature hits 200°F (93°C). Let it rest for 30 to 60 minutes. After the pork is done resting, shred it using two forks or meat shredders. Add 1 to 2 cups (240 to 480 ml) of barbecue sauce to the shredded pork, depending on the consistency you prefer.

In a large bowl, combine the cabbage, pineapple, cilantro, mayonnaise, apple cider vinegar, honey, salt and pepper. Give it a mix, making sure all the ingredients are coated with the dressing. Adjust the seasoning to your preference after tasting.

Now we can build the sandwich. Grab a hamburger bun and place a generous amount of the finished pulled pork on the bottom bun. Next, add some pineapple slaw on top of the pulled pork, top with the bun and enjoy.

MAPLE-GLAZED PORK TENDERLOIN

Yield: 4–5 servings

The tenderloin from most animals is considered to be a prize cut and often the most expensive by weight. Pork tenderloin always intrigued me due to its affordability, and if you know how to cook it you will have one of the most tender bites of food in your life. To get the perfect pork tenderloin, I like to give the pork a quick sear to lock in flavor immediately, and then I roast it in the oven with a delicious glaze to infuse it with a ton of additional flavor. This tenderloin recipe is salty and savory with a touch of sweetness that works perfectly with this cut of meat.

¼ cup (60 ml) maple syrup

2 tbsp (30 ml) Dijon mustard

2 tbsp (30 ml) soy sauce

2 cloves garlic, minced

1 tsp dried thyme

½ tsp black pepper

½ tsp salt

2 (1 lb [454 g]) pork tenderloins

1 tbsp (15 ml) olive oil

Roasted vegetables or mashed potatoes, for serving

Preheat the oven to 375°F (190°C)

In a small bowl, whisk together the maple syrup, mustard, soy sauce, garlic, thyme, pepper and salt and set aside while you sear the tenderloins.

Pat the tenderloins dry using paper towels—this will make sure you get a perfect sear. In an oven-safe skillet or frying pan, heat the olive oil over medium-high heat. Once the oil is shimmering, add the tenderloins to the pan and sear them for 2 to 3 minutes per side. We're looking for a golden-brown crust here. Remove the skillet from the heat and brush the glaze over the pork tenderloins, coating them both evenly. Make sure to use plenty of the glaze here as it will really pull through in the end result.

Transfer the skillet with the pork tenderloins to the pre-heated oven. Roast for 15 to 20 minutes, or until the internal temperature reaches 140°F (60°C). While they rest for 5 to 10 minutes, you are looking for the temperature to hit 145°F (63°C). Now, it's time to slice the pork tenderloins and drizzle any remaining glaze from the skillet over the slices, adding a bunch of additional flavor. Serve with roasted vegetables which pair up perfectly with this.

SPICY THAI BASIL BEEF STIR-FRY

Yield: 2–3 servings

One of the best dishes that gives you plenty of room to experiment with flavor is a good ol' stir-fry. If you are a follower of my social media channels, it's no surprise I'm a beef and steak kind of guy. I am always trying to find new ways to spice it up, and this Spicy Thai Basil Beef Stir-Fry is a wonderful take on a classic stir-fry. We build the flavor one layer at time while we quickly cook the beef, vegetables, sauce and aromatics over high heat. A lot of stir-fries I've had feel like a boring mash-up of ingredients just tossed in a pan, while this recipe delivers by really building depth of flavor, from the first bite to the last. This is best served over jasmine rice with a squeeze of lime juice.

2 tbsp (30 ml) soy sauce

1 tbsp (15 ml) oyster sauce

1 tbsp (15 ml) fish sauce

1 tsp sugar

½ tsp black pepper

2 tbsp (30 ml) avocado oil

3 cloves garlic, minced

1 red chile pepper, thinly sliced

1 lb (454 g) beef sirloin or flank steak, thinly sliced

1 red or green bell pepper, thinly sliced

1 onion, thinly sliced

1 cup (24 g) fresh basil leaves

Cooked jasmine rice, for serving

Lime wedges, for serving

In a small bowl, combine the soy sauce, oyster sauce, fish sauce, sugar and pepper. Stir well to create your sauce mixture, and then set it aside.

Heat the avocado oil in a large skillet or wok over high heat. Once the oil is hot, add the garlic and sliced chile pepper. Stir-fry for 30 seconds, or until aromatic. Now, it's time to add the beef to the skillet. Stir-fry the beef for 2 to 3 minutes, or until it browns and reaches your desired level of doneness. Once cooked, remove the beef from the skillet and set it aside.

In the same skillet, add the bell pepper and onion. Stir-fry for 2 minutes, or until they start to soften but still retain a crunch. Return the cooked beef to the skillet, and pour the sauce mixture over the beef and veggies. Stir-fry for 1 to 2 minutes, allowing the sauce to coat every ingredient in the skillet. Take the skillet off the heat, add the basil and toss everything together. The residual heat will wilt the basil leaves, which gives the dish a ton of additional flavor.

Serve over cooked jasmine rice and garnish the dish with lime wedges on the side. Squeeze the lime over the stir-fry to add a refreshing layer of additional flavor and enjoy.

QUINOA-STUFFED PEPPERS WITH SUN-DRIED TOMATO SAUCE

Yield: 4 stuffed peppers

Growing up, stuffed bell peppers made a regular appearance at my dinner table. Both my mother and grandmother had great recipes that were considered more traditional. I still love making their versions to this day, but my love of pushing back on traditional boundaries in the kitchen led me to this recipe. Quinoa takes the place of rice, which gives us a better texture in the end, along with incredible flavor to pair with the filling. Ingredients such as carrots, zucchini, corn and black beans bring both flavor and texture that you'll never find in a traditional stuffed pepper recipe. It's topped off with a sun-dried tomato sauce that perfectly complements this Mediterranean twist on a childhood favorite of mine.

For the Quinoa

2 cups (475 ml) vegetable broth or water

1 cup (180 g) rinsed quinoa

For the Stuffing

1 tbsp (15 ml) olive oil

1 onion, diced

2 cloves garlic, minced

1 zucchini, diced

1 carrot, diced

½ cup (85 g) corn kernels (fresh or frozen)

½ cup (85 g) drained and rinsed canned black beans

½ cup (85 g) diced tomatoes

¼ cup (15 g) chopped fresh parsley

1 tsp dried oregano

½ tsp ground cumin

Salt and black pepper, as needed

Preheat the oven to 375°F (190°C).

To make the quinoa, in a medium-sized saucepan, bring the vegetable broth to a boil. Add the quinoa, reduce the heat to low, cover and let it simmer for 15 minutes, or until the quinoa is cooked and all the liquid has been absorbed. Remove it from the heat and set aside.

To make the stuffing, heat the olive oil in a large skillet over medium heat. Add the onion and garlic and sauté for 2 to 3 minutes, or until the onion becomes translucent and softens. Add the zucchini, carrot, corn, black beans, tomatoes, parsley, oregano, cumin, salt and pepper to the skillet. Allow the mixture to cook for 5 to 7 minutes.

For the Sun-Dried Tomato Sauce

½ cup (75 g) drained sun-dried tomatoes (packed in oil)

¼ cup (60 g) tomato paste

2 tbsp (30 ml) olive oil

2 cloves garlic

1 tbsp (15 ml) balsamic vinegar

¼ cup (60 ml) water

Salt and black pepper, to taste

For the Peppers

4 bell peppers, tops and seeds removed

To make the sauce, grab a blender or food processor and combine the sun-dried tomatoes, tomato paste, olive oil, garlic, balsamic vinegar, water, salt and pepper. Blend until the sauce is smooth and set aside.

To make the peppers, in a large mixing bowl, combine the cooked quinoa and the sautéed vegetable mixture. Give it a good stir, and then you are ready to stuff the peppers. Gently press the quinoa and vegetable mixture into each pepper until they are fully packed. Arrange them standing up in a baking dish and pour the sun-dried tomato sauce over them. Cover the baking dish with foil and let the magic happen in the oven. Bake for 30 to 35 minutes, or until the peppers are tender and cooked through. Remove the foil and let the peppers cook an extra 5 minutes, allowing the tops to get slightly brown. Allow the stuffed peppers to cool for a few minutes before serving. This take on a classic dinnertime meal is one that takes what you know as a stuffed pepper to an entirely new level.

CAPRESE-STUFFED CHICKEN BREAST

Yield: 2 stuffed chicken breasts

Caprese is more than just a delicious appetizer or side; it can be a key piece of the entrée as well. Stuffed chicken is the perfect vessel for tying in the bright and fresh flavors that are traditionally found in caprese. This is the best version of stuffed chicken I've tried yet, since the stuffing seasons the meat from the inside as well as guarantees a perfectly juicy end result. This recipe takes what some consider a bland protein and puts it center stage to show you why that is not the case here.

2 (400–450 g) boneless, skinless chicken breasts

Salt and black pepper, as needed

4 slices fresh mozzarella cheese

4 slices tomato

8 fresh basil leaves, plus more for garnishing

1 tbsp (15 ml) olive oil

2 tbsp (30 ml) balsamic glaze

Preheat the oven to 400°F (204°C).

Butterfly the chicken breasts by making a horizontal cut through the thickest part of each piece, making sure not to cut all the way through. Open the chicken breasts at the seam to prepare them for the stuffing.

Season both sides of the chicken breasts with salt and pepper. On one side of the butterflied chicken breast, place two slices of the mozzarella, two slices of tomato and four fresh basil leaves. Fold the other side of each chicken breast over the filling, trying your best to seal everything inside.

Heat the olive oil in an oven-safe skillet over medium-high heat. Once the oil is hot, carefully place the stuffed chicken breasts in the skillet and let them sear for 3 to 4 minutes on each side, or until they are browned. Transfer the skillet to the preheated oven. Let the chicken breasts bake for 15 to 20 minutes, or until they are cooked through and reach an internal temperature of 165°F (75°C). Remove the skillet from the oven and let the chicken rest for 5 minutes.

Drizzle the balsamic glaze over the stuffed chicken breasts, garnish with more fresh basil and enjoy a fun take on stuffed chicken that is sure to be a hit with the entire family.

PERFECTING PIZZA IN THE SKILLET

I have had a passion for great pizza and what exactly makes it great for over fifteen years. Through trial and error, I have really nailed down the perfect pizza dough and pizza sauce recipe to go along with these incredibly unique pizzas. You won't find your basic pepperoni pizza here (even though I do enjoy them too), but you will find some amazing next-level flavor combinations. The Fresh Fig and Caramelized Onion Pizza (page 38) will blow your palate away from the very first bite, while the Blackberry Ricotta Pizza (page 46) will always deliver as the perfect sweet and savory treat. Let's break out your cast-iron skillet and make some unforgettable pizza.

MY FAVORITE DOUGH RECIPE

Yield: 2-4 dough balls

When it comes to making an amazing pizza, you must start with an amazing dough. I love pizza so much because it can always be elevated beyond the standard. My first job in the culinary space was at a local pizza shop, and that's where I became obsessed with perfecting the core piece of every pizza: the dough. With this dough recipe, it's all about technique and quality ingredients. We're about to create a perfect canvas for your favorite pizza, and this dough will give you the buttery, crispy crust that makes a pan pizza the best.

2¼ cups (270 g) all-purpose flour

1 tsp instant yeast

1 tsp sugar

1 tsp salt

1 tbsp (15 ml) olive oil, plus more for drizzling

¾ cup (180 ml) warm water

In a large bowl, combine the flour, yeast, sugar and salt. Give it a quick mix to evenly distribute the dry ingredients. Create a well in the center, and add the olive oil and water. Stir the ingredients together until a shaggy dough forms. Transfer the dough onto a lightly floured surface.

Now comes the fun part—kneading. Gently knead the dough for 5 to 7 minutes, or until it becomes smooth and elastic. Remember, kneading develops the gluten for a chewy texture.

Shape the dough into a ball and place it back into the bowl. Drizzle olive oil over the dough and cover it with a clean kitchen towel. Let it rise in a warm spot for 1 to 2 hours, or until it doubles in size.

Once the dough has risen, gently punch it down to release air bubbles.

Then divide the dough into two to four equal portions and form each of them into a ball. The number of dough balls just depends on your desired thickness and size. Now you are ready to create a masterpiece using your favorite sauce, cheese and toppings . . . or even better, try one of my favorite elevated pizza recipes in this chapter.

SAN MARZANO PIZZA SAUCE

Yield: 4 cups (950 ml)

A quality pizza sauce is just as important as the dough when you really want your pizzas to stand out. Pizza sauce at its core is simple to make, but the best tasting sauce requires attention to detail alongside quality ingredients. With only six to seven ingredients, it's important to make sure that you use the best quality ingredients available to you if you really want the flavors to shine through. For example, using San Marzano tomatoes makes a noticeable difference due to being much less acidic than other popular tomatoes. Creating the perfect sauce starts with building intentional layers of flavor with well-seasoned aromatic ingredients, and you'll find that in full force here.

2 tbsp (30 ml) extra virgin olive oil

3 cloves garlic, minced

1 (28-oz [794-g]) can crushed San Marzano tomatoes

1 tsp salt

1 tsp dried oregano

¼ tsp black pepper

¼ tsp crushed red pepper flakes (optional)

Heat the olive oil in a saucepan over medium heat. Once the oil is warmed up, add the garlic and sauté for 1 to 2 minutes, or until it becomes fragrant and releases a salivating aroma. Add the can of crushed tomatoes and give it a good stir to help the flavors start to come together. Sprinkle in the salt, oregano, pepper, and if you like a little heat, the crushed red pepper flakes. Stir everything together, making sure all the ingredients are well combined. Allow the sauce to come to a gentle simmer and cook for 10 to 15 minutes, stirring occasionally. This will allow the flavors to meld and the sauce to thicken slightly.

Once the sauce has simmered to perfection, remove it from the heat and let it cool slightly. Feel free to adjust the seasonings to your taste. You can add more or less of any ingredient to personalize the sauce just the way you like it. This recipe yields enough sauce for two large pizzas or three to four small pizzas, depending on how saucy you like it. This sauce can also be stored in an airtight container in the refrigerator for up to one week.

PROSCIUTTO DI PARMA PIZZA

Yield: 3-4 servings

Prosciutto and pizza truly are a match made in heaven. I came up with this recipe when I was looking for a way to really elevate pizza using one of my favorite ingredients: prosciutto di Parma. Combining the rich and savory flavors of prosciutto, tangy goat cheese and peppery arugula results in a culinary masterpiece that transports you to the heart of Italy with each bite. Combinations like this raise the question: Does the perfect pizza exist? This recipe might just give you the answer, and don't be shocked when this becomes a mainstay for pizza night in your home (it is in mine).

1–2 tbsp (15–30 ml) melted unsalted butter

1 lb (454 g) My Favorite Dough Recipe (page 33)

½ cup (120 ml) San Marzano Pizza Sauce (page 34)

½ cup (20 g) arugula

6 pieces prosciutto di Parma

½ cup (70 g) goat cheese crumbles

8 oz (226 g) shredded mozzarella, divided

1 Campari or Roma tomato, sliced ⅛–¼" (3–6 mm) thick

Fresh cracked pepper, to taste

To kick things off, preheat the oven to 500°F (260°C). (Whether you use a cast-iron skillet or a pizza stone, temperature is key to getting that perfect crust.)

Grab a brush and generously coat the inside of a cast-iron skillet with the melted butter. The butter will add amazing depth of flavor to the crust as well as help it get perfectly golden. Stretch out the dough evenly to fit in the skillet, aiming for a 12-inch (30-cm) diameter. Use a fork to gently poke holes in the dough to avoid bubbles during the cook.

Spread down a layer of the pizza sauce on the dough, leaving a ½- to ¾-inch (1.3- to 2-cm) space uncovered around the edges. Next up, it's time to add the arugula. Distribute it evenly across the sauce before you add the star of the show: the prosciutto di Parma. Bunch each prosciutto slice up into a loose ball and flatten it slightly, and then place them across the pizza, making sure the slices are evenly spaced. Sprinkle the goat cheese crumbles over the entire pizza, followed by 4 oz (113 g) of the shredded mozzarella. Then we can introduce the sliced tomatoes into the mix, nestling them between the prosciutto slices. Top it off with the remaining mozzarella.

Pop the pizza in the oven and bake for 15 to 20 minutes, or until the crust reaches a glorious golden-brown hue and the cheese is melted. Once the pizza is out of the oven, allow it to cool slightly in the pan. Finish it off with a sprinkle of freshly ground pepper for an added kick and aroma that will elevate the flavors even more. This is truly a beautiful pizza and tastes even better than it looks. Cut the pizza into eight equally delicious slices and get ready to savor every moment. This Prosciutto di Parma Pizza is meant to be enjoyed and shared, so gather your loved ones and indulge in this slice of Italy.

FRESH FIG AND CARAMELIZED ONION PIZZA

Yield: 3–4 servings

Figs are one of the last ingredients people think of when it comes to pizza. It's by no means as controversial as pineapple, and once you wrap your taste buds around a slice of this, you will want to share the recipe with all your family and friends. When you take the time to caramelize onions, you need to complement them with amazing ingredients. The fresh figs bring a bright sweetness, the pancetta adds the salty touch we all want and the combination of the creamy goat cheese and vibrant arugula take it to the next level.

Caramelized Onions

1 tbsp (14 g) unsalted butter

1 tbsp (15 ml) olive oil

½ large onion, thinly sliced

½ tsp salt

½ tsp black pepper

Pizza

2 tbsp (30 ml) melted unsalted butter, divided

4 oz (113 g) diced pancetta

1 lb (454 g) My Favorite Dough Recipe (page 33)

2 tbsp (30 ml) olive oil

8 oz (226 g) shredded mozzarella

3–4 fresh figs, sliced ⅛-inch (3-mm) thick

4 oz (113 g) diced pancetta

½ cup (75 g) crumbled goat cheese

Fresh cracked pepper

¼ cup (10 g) arugula

In a large skillet, melt the butter with the olive oil over medium-low heat. Add the onions and season with salt and pepper while stirring to coat with the butter and oil. Cook the onions for 30 to 35 minutes while stirring occasionally. They will start to caramelize and turn golden brown, and they will finish up caramelizing while they cook on top of the pizza. Set the onions aside to cool slightly while we prepare the rest of the pizza.

Preheat the oven to a toasty 500°F (260°C). Brush the inside of a cast-iron skillet with 1 tablespoon (15 ml) of the melted butter to add an extra layer of flavor to your crust. In a small pan, add the remaining butter and panfry the diced pancetta until slightly crispy. Set it aside.

Stretch out the pizza dough evenly to fit the cast-iron skillet, aiming for a 12-inch (30-cm) diameter. Use a fork to gently poke holes in the dough to avoid bubbles during the cook. Brush the olive oil onto the dough, ensuring an even distribution to enhance the taste. Sprinkle the mozzarella over the entire pizza, spreading it all the way to the edge. Then place the figs on the pizza, spacing them 1 inch (2.5 cm) apart. Spread the caramelized onions between the figs, adding pockets of rich, sweet flavor throughout. Sprinkle the diced pancetta and crumbled goat cheese on top, creating a delightful combination of savory and creamy elements.

Slide the pizza in the oven and bake for 15 to 20 minutes, or until the cheese is melted throughout and the crust becomes irresistibly crispy. Once the pizza is out of the oven, allow it to cool slightly in the pan before you remove it. Now, it's time for the finishing touches. Sprinkle some pepper over the pizza, and scatter a handful of vibrant arugula leaves on top, bringing a refreshing touch that ties everything together.

BUTTER CHICKEN PIZZA WITH NAAN CRUST

Yield: 2 servings

This pizza is the fusion of flavors you need in your life. This twist on a classic dish brings all the aromatic spices of butter chicken and crispy naan crust to the comforting world of pizza. The rich and creamy tomato-based sauce, tender chicken pieces and a hint of heat will have you questioning why this is not in every pizza shop around. As someone who is of Middle Eastern descent, I love my spices and bold flavors, and each bite of this dish is a burst of Indian-inspired deliciousness. Get ready to savor the incredible marriage of Indian cuisine and Italian flare in what's become one of my favorite pizza creations.

1 tbsp (15 ml) vegetable oil

2–3 boneless, skinless chicken thighs, cut into bite-sized pieces

½ cup (113 g) unsalted butter

1 onion, finely chopped

3 cloves garlic, minced

1 tbsp (15 g) grated ginger

1 tsp ground cumin

1 tsp ground coriander

1 tsp paprika

½ tsp turmeric

¼ tsp cayenne pepper

1 (14-oz [397-g]) can tomato purée

½ cup (120 ml) heavy cream

Salt and pepper, to taste

1 (2-pack) premade naan bread

½ cup (57 g) shredded mozzarella cheese

¼ cup (40 g) chopped red onion

¼ cup (15 g) chopped fresh cilantro

Preheat the oven to 425°F (218°C).

In a large skillet, heat the vegetable oil over medium-high heat. Add the chicken and cook for 6 to 7 minutes, or until it's browned on all sides and cooked through. Set it aside.

Using the same skillet, melt the butter over medium heat. Add the onion, garlic and ginger. Cook for 2 to 3 minutes, or until the onion softens and turns translucent. Sprinkle in the cumin, coriander, paprika, turmeric and cayenne pepper. Give it a good stir and let the spices cook for 1 to 2 minutes, allowing their flavors to develop. Mix in the tomato purée and simmer for 5 to 7 minutes, allowing the sauce to thicken and intensify in flavor.

Return the chicken to the skillet and mix it with the sauce. Cook the mixture for 2 to 3 minutes, or until the chicken is heated through and thoroughly coated. Pour in the heavy cream and stir it into the mixture. Cook for 1 to 2 minutes, or until the sauce thickens, enveloping the chicken in one of the most aromatic sauces out there. Season with salt and pepper. Set it aside to cool for 10 to 15 minutes.

Place the naan bread in a cast-iron skillet or on a baking sheet, and once the butter chicken sauce is cooled off, spoon the mixture over the naan. Sprinkle the shredded mozzarella cheese over the sauce, followed by the chopped red onion. Slide the pizza into the preheated oven and bake for 10 to 12 minutes, or until the cheese melts and the edges crisp up. Once out of the oven, allow the pizza to cool for a few minutes. Before slicing and serving, garnish it with a sprinkle of fresh chopped cilantro. There you have it. Your Butter Chicken Pizza with Naan Crust is ready to be devoured.

THAI GREEN CURRY SHRIMP PIZZA

Yield: 3–4 servings

When I'm trying to come up with new ideas for unique pizzas, I love taking inspiration from dishes I love from across the world. This one is a true fusion of Thai and Italian cuisines that results in the best way to use seafood on a pizza. I've tried crab and lobster on pizza before, but when shrimp is done right and paired with Thai green curry it has the best texture to complement a pizza. I have always believed that pizza can cross into any form of fusion cuisine and come out the other side as an amazing creation that checks all the boxes.

For the Shrimp

2 tbsp (28 g) unsalted butter

1 cup (150 g) raw peeled and deveined shrimp

Salt and pepper, as needed

For the Sauce

1 tbsp (15 g) Thai green curry paste

¼ cup (60 ml) coconut milk

For the Pizza

2 tbsp (30 ml) melted butter

1 lb (454 g) My Favorite Dough Recipe (page 33)

½ cup (75 g) sliced red bell pepper

½ cup (75 g) sliced red onion

½ cup (57 g) shredded mozzarella cheese

¼ cup (15 g) chopped fresh cilantro

¼ cup (35 g) chopped roasted peanuts (optional)

Lime wedges, for serving

Preheat the oven to 500°F (260°C).

To make the shrimp, in a large skillet, melt the butter over medium heat. Season the shrimp with salt and pepper and add them to the skillet. Cook for 1½ to 2 minutes per side, or until they are almost cooked through. Set them aside to cool slightly.

To make the sauce, in a small bowl, whisk together the Thai green curry paste and coconut milk until you have a smooth and flavorful sauce. Set it aside for now.

Now, let's prepare the pizza crust. Brush the melted butter on the inside of a cast-iron skillet for that crispy, buttery base. Stretch the pizza dough evenly to fit the pan, aiming for a 12-inch (30-cm) diameter. Use a fork to gently poke holes in the dough to avoid bubbles during the cook.

Time to layer on the flavors. Spread the curry paste mixture evenly over the pizza dough. Next, place the semi-cooked shrimp on top of the curry sauce, followed by the bell pepper and red onion. Sprinkle the mozzarella evenly over the top of the pizza and all the way to the edge. Slide the pizza into the preheated oven and bake for 15 to 20 minutes, or until the cheese is melted and crispy along the edges. Once the pizza emerges from the oven, let it cool in the pan for 5 minutes. Then sprinkle it with the cilantro and roasted peanuts for an extra burst of flavor and texture (the peanuts are optional, but highly recommended). Serve the pizza with lime wedges on the side, allowing each guest to take their slice up a notch if preferred.

SAVORY SOUTH OF THE BORDER PIZZA

Yield: 3–4 servings

If it was up to me, I'd eat chorizo every day. It's one of my favorite proteins to cook with and use outside of its traditional recipes. When it comes to pizza, you always want a great balance of salty, savory and spicy, and chorizo is one ingredient that gets that job done and then some. This recipe borrows from a traditional Hispanic chorizo and potato dish called papas con chorizo to create the ultimate south of the border fusion pizza. It's a carb-loaded, spicy and flavor-packed meal that is perfect for breakfast, brunch or lunch.

1 tbsp (15 ml) olive oil

6–8 oz (170–226 g) chorizo

1 cup (150 g) diced russet potatoes

½ tsp paprika

½ tsp garlic powder

Salt and pepper, as needed

1–2 tbsp (15–30 ml) melted butter

1 lb (454 g) My Favorite Dough Recipe (page 33)

½ cup (120 ml) San Marzano Pizza Sauce (page 34)

8 oz (226 g) shredded mozzarella cheese, divided

4 oz (113 g) queso fresco

Fresh cilantro, chopped

Heat the olive oil in a large skillet over medium-high heat. Add the chorizo, breaking it apart as it starts to brown. After 2 to 3 minutes, add the potatoes. Sprinkle in the paprika, garlic, salt and pepper, giving everything a good mix. Stir and cook for 6 to 8 minutes, or until the chorizo is cooked through and the potatoes are nicely browned.

Preheat the oven to 500°F (260°C).

Brush the inside of a cast-iron skillet with the melted butter. Stretch the pizza dough evenly to fit the pan, aiming for a 12-inch (30-cm) diameter. Use a fork to gently poke holes in the dough to avoid bubbles during the cook. Spread the pizza sauce evenly over the crust. Sprinkle two-thirds of the grated mozzarella cheese over the sauce. Add the chorizo on top of the cheese, spreading it evenly. Then fill the gaps by spreading a generous amount of the potatoes. Top it with the remaining mozzarella cheese, slide the pizza into the preheated oven and bake for 15 to 20 minutes.

Once the pizza emerges from the oven, sprinkle it with queso fresco and a generous amount of fresh cilantro. Now, slice it up, grab a piece and enjoy one of the best combinations of flavors out there in a new way. The rich and spicy chorizo, the crispy potatoes and the irresistible blend of cheeses will be a hit next pizza night.

BLACKBERRY RICOTTA PIZZA

Yield: 3–4 servings

I love dessert pizza, but, then again, who doesn't? Most pizza shops around me only have apple or cherry versions if any at all. This sweet and savory pizza is really one of a kind and the best version of a dessert pizza I've tasted. The nutty, creamy and herbal flavors you achieve with the cheese mixture lays the foundation for pops of refreshing flavor from the smashed blackberries. When it comes to berries, blackberries are much more robust in flavor and scent when compared to others, and they pair up perfectly with the crunch from the chopped walnuts and the sweet aromatic finish from the honey and basil.

1 cup (240 g) ricotta cheese

¼ cup (25 g) grated Parmesan cheese

½ tsp dried thyme or oregano

Salt and pepper, to taste

1–2 tbsp (15–30 ml) melted butter

1 lb (454 g) My Favorite Dough Recipe (page 33)

1 cup (150 g) smashed blackberries

¼ cup (30 g) chopped walnuts

Honey, for drizzling

Fresh basil leaves, for garnishing

Preheat the oven to 500°F (260°C).

In a small bowl, mix the ricotta cheese, Parmesan cheese and thyme, and season with salt and pepper. This delicious mixture will be the base of our pizza.

Brush the inside of a cast-iron skillet with the melted butter. Stretch the pizza dough evenly to fit the pan, aiming for a 12-inch (30-cm) diameter. Use a fork to gently poke holes in the dough to avoid bubbles during the cook. Spread the cheese mixture evenly over the crust, leaving a ½- to ¾-inch (1.3- to 2-cm) space around the edge. Sprinkle the blackberries and the walnuts on top of the cheese, creating a perfect balance of sweetness and crunch.

Slide the pizza into the preheated oven and bake for 15 to 20 minutes, or until the crust takes on a golden-brown color.

Once the pizza is out of the oven, drizzle it with honey, adding a touch of natural sweetness that complements these flavors perfectly. Finish off the pizza by garnishing it with fresh basil leaves, adding a pop of freshness.

SHOW-STOPPING SIDES

We can't forget about the support system of a great meal—or the true stars of most cookouts—the sides. A great side dish can improve the overall meal in a big way, and I love trying to make the side dishes stand out just as much as the main courses. In this chapter, I've included my Middle Eastern Caprese Salad (page 72) that is inspired by my heritage. You'll also get a chance to make my Smoked Paprika and Cheddar Corn Bread with Honey Butter (page 71), which will change your life by incorporating a beautifully smoky flavor to a classic barbecue staple. Whether you are making a meal for yourself or tasked with bringing a side to your next cookout, this chapter will give you options that are guaranteed to be a hit and put a new spin on your favorites.

GARLIC-HERB HASSELBACK POTATOES WITH GRUYÈRE

Yield: 4 servings

The first time I made Hasselback potatoes was for my social media page, shortly after I first started creating videos. I have tried so many variations while trying to perfect it, and my favorite version yet is this one right here. The unique way the potatoes are sliced to create room for tons of additional flavor puts any normal baked potato to shame. The garlic butter with herbs adds a beautiful touch, but the real standout is the Gruyère cheese, which adds a richness alongside its naturally nutty flavor. Next time you are looking for the perfect potato side dish, make these, and be prepared to add this to your list of go-to sides.

4 large russet potatoes

6 tbsp (90 ml) melted butter

5 cloves garlic, minced

2 tbsp (8 g) finely chopped fresh parsley

1 tbsp (2 g) fresh thyme leaves

Salt and pepper, to taste

1½ cups (150 g) shredded Gruyère cheese

Sour cream and diced chives, for garnishing (optional)

Preheat the oven to 400°F (204°C), and line a baking sheet with parchment paper.

To prepare the potatoes, wash them and give them a good scrub, ensuring they're clean, and then dry them off. To prevent cutting all the way through, place each potato on a cutting board between two chopsticks or wooden spoons. With a sharp knife, carefully cut thin slices along the length of each potato, ⅛ to ¼ inch (3 to 6 mm) apart. Keep cutting until the knife hits the chopsticks or spoons. Repeat this process for all the potatoes, and set them aside.

In a small bowl, combine the melted butter, garlic, parsley, thyme, salt and pepper. Mix everything together to create a delicious garlic and herb butter. Generously brush the butter mixture over the potatoes, making sure it gets into all the slices. Place the potatoes on the prepared baking sheet and pop them into the preheated oven. Bake for 40 to 50 minutes, or until they turn golden brown, crispy on the outside and tender on the inside.

Take potatoes out of the oven and sprinkle the shredded cheese on top. Evenly spread the cheese over the potatoes and return them to the oven for 3 to 5 minutes or until the cheese is melted and bubbly. Remove the potatoes from the oven and let them cool for a few minutes. Top them off with an optional dollop of sour cream and diced chives, and they are ready to serve.

FRESH HERBED COUSCOUS

Yield: 3–4 servings

Couscous packed with fresh herbs and vegetables may just be the most refreshing summer cookout side. The nice pop of flavors from the fresh herbs, crunchy vegetables and lemon dressing makes this dish an amazing addition to any meal. Keep it simple with the dressing, and let the flavors work together to give this dish a new spin. This is even great on its own as a light and refreshing meal.

1¼ cups (295 ml) vegetable or chicken broth

1 cup (180 g) couscous

2 tbsp (8 g) finely chopped fresh parsley

2 tbsp (8 g) finely chopped fresh mint

2 tbsp (8 g) finely chopped fresh cilantro

2 green onions, thinly sliced

¼ cup (30 g) finely diced red bell pepper

¼ cup (30 g) finely diced yellow bell pepper

¼ cup (40 g) finely diced cucumber

2 tbsp (30 ml) lemon juice

2 tbsp (30 ml) extra virgin olive oil

Salt and pepper, to taste

Bring the vegetable broth to a boil in a medium saucepan. Remove the saucepan from heat and stir in the couscous. Cover the saucepan and let it sit for 5 minutes, allowing the couscous to absorb all the liquid. Using a fork, fluff the cooked couscous and transfer it to a large mixing bowl. Let it cool slightly for 3 to 5 minutes. Add the parsley, mint, cilantro, green onions, bell peppers and cucumber to the couscous. Mix everything well to ensure the flavors are evenly distributed.

In a small bowl, whisk together the lemon juice, olive oil, salt and pepper to create a tangy and zesty dressing. Drizzle the lemon dressing over the couscous mixture and give it a good toss, making sure all the couscous and vegetables are coated with the dressing. Adjust the seasoning to your preference. Allow it to sit for 10 to 15 minutes, letting the flavors pull together even more and letting the couscous absorb the dressing. Then you can serve up this refreshing and flavor-packed side with your favorite entrée.

PARMESAN AND ROASTED GARLIC MASHED POTATOES

Yield: 6–8 servings

Mashed potatoes are near the top of the list for almost everyone when it comes to comfort food, but not all mashed potato recipes are created equal. The type of potato used has one of the largest impacts, so you want to use a potato with a higher starch content such as Yukon Gold or russet. Here, Yukon Gold potatoes lay the foundation for the buttery smooth texture, combined with the nutty aromatic flavor of roasted garlic and freshly grated Parmesan cheese. Let's get to peeling some potatoes and start making the ultimate mashed potato side.

8–10 cloves garlic, peeled

½–⅔ cup (120–160 ml) olive oil

½ tsp salt, plus more to taste

½ tsp pepper, plus more to taste

3 lb (1.4 kg) Yukon Gold potatoes, peeled and cubed

½ cup (120 ml) whole milk

½ cup (55 g) grated Parmesan cheese

3 tbsp (45 g) unsalted butter

Preheat the oven to 325°F (163°C).

Place the garlic cloves in a small baking dish and cover them with the olive oil. Season the oil and garlic with salt and pepper before placing in the oven. Bake for 1 hour. This slow roasting process is often referred to as making garlic confit, and it completely transforms the garlic by slow roasting it in olive oil. When the garlic is 20 minutes away from being done, bring a large pot of salted water to a boil over medium-high heat. Add the potatoes and cook for 15 to 20 minutes, or until fork tender.

Remove the baking dish from the oven and let it sit while the potatoes finish up. When the potatoes are done, strain them and place them back in the pot used to cook them. You can mash these by hand with a potato masher, but I recommend using a potato ricer if you have one in order to get the smoothest consistency possible.

Transfer the potatoes to a large mixing bowl, and mix in the garlic, milk, Parmesan and butter. Once you have a creamy final product, taste for salt and pepper and season accordingly. These potatoes are silky, filled with robust flavors and worth taking the time to make for your next meal.

GRILLED CORN WITH CHILI LIME BUTTER AND COTIJA CHEESE

Yield: 4 corncobs

It really doesn't get much easier than grilled corn on the cob, but don't let that stop you from punching up the flavor. I love the way chili powder and lime complement corn, and this dish almost tastes like you are eating corn salsa right off the cob. After grilling up the corn next to your favorite grilled entrée, you'll brush on a flavorful butter and add some cotija cheese and cilantro to pull it all together. This one is a simple, flavorful staple during grilling season at my house.

4 tbsp (56 g) softened unsalted butter

1 tsp chili powder

Zest of 1 lime

Juice of 1 lime

Pinch of salt, plus more to taste

4 corncobs, husked

¼ cup (28 g) crumbled cotija cheese or queso fresco

Chopped fresh cilantro, for garnishing

Preheat your grill to medium-high heat.

In a small bowl, combine the butter, chili powder, lime zest, lime juice and salt until smooth. Set aside to develop while we cook the corn.

Place the corncobs on the preheated grill and cook for 10 to 12 minutes, turning them every 3 to 4 minutes. We're looking for tender corn with a nice hint of char. Once the corncobs are cooked through, remove them from the grill and allow them to cool slightly. We want them to be cool enough to eat, but still warm enough to melt the butter.

Using a brush or a knife, evenly spread the chili lime butter over each corncob. Sprinkle the crumbled cotija cheese over the buttered corn alongside the cilantro. This is the definition of a simple but show-stopping side dish that will steal the spotlight at your next cookout. The sweet and smoky flavors of the corn, combined with the incredible butter, make for an amazing bite of food.

DOUBLE-SMOKED MAC AND CHEESE WITH BACON

Yield: 6–8 servings

When I first got into smoking meats on my pellet grill, I dove right into what sides would work best on it and landed on this incredible version of smoked mac and cheese. I've always loved mac and cheese, and after making tweaks to this recipe over the years, I have dialed in what I consider to be the best smoked mac around. It's creamy, cheesy and of course the bacon just takes it up another notch. Using a smoker for this recipe to infuse flavor every step of the way really sets this apart.

For the Sauce

2 cups (480 ml) half-and-half

1 cup (240 ml) whole milk

8 oz (226 g) cream cheese, cubed and softened

4 tbsp (56 g) unsalted butter

1 tsp dry mustard

2 tsp (10 ml) hot sauce

1 tsp black pepper

½ tsp cayenne pepper

1 tsp smoked paprika, plus extra for garnishing

For the Mac and Cheese

1 lb (454 g) dried cavatappi or elbow macaroni

1 cup (113 g) shredded mozzarella cheese

1 cup (113 g) shredded smoked mild cheddar cheese

1 cup (113 g) shredded smoked Gouda cheese

6 pieces of cooked bacon, chopped

1 cup (90 g) panko breadcrumbs

¼ cup (25 g) grated Parmesan cheese

2 tbsp (30 ml) melted butter

Chopped fresh parsley, for garnishing (optional)

Preheat your smoker to 225°F (107°C) and grease a 12-inch (30-cm) cast-iron skillet.

Mix together the half-and-half, milk, cream cheese, butter, mustard, hot sauce, pepper, cayenne and smoked paprika in the cast-iron skillet, and then place on the smoker for 45 minutes. While that smokes, cook the pasta according to the package instructions until just before al dente. Drain the pasta. In a large mixing bowl or the pot used to cook the pasta, add the mozzarella, cheddar, Gouda, bacon and pasta. Stir to combine.

When the sauce mixture is done, remove it from the smoker, and then turn the smoker up to 325°F (163°C). Whisk the sauce until it's smooth. Then combine the sauce with the cheese and pasta mixture and stir once more until everything is spread throughout. Transfer everything back to the cast-iron skillet.

In a small bowl, mix together the breadcrumbs, Parmesan cheese and melted butter. Then sprinkle the buttered panko breadcrumbs evenly over the top of the mac and cheese. Return the cast-iron skillet to the smoker and let it cook for 40 to 45 minutes, or until the mac and cheese is bubbly and the top is golden brown. Remove it from the smoker and top it off with additional smoked paprika and chopped parsley (if using) before serving.

GAME-CHANGING GARLIC BREAD

Yield: 6–8 servings

Who doesn't love garlic bread with their favorite pasta dish or pizza? With my background in making pizza, I spent quite a bit of time learning to perfect garlic bread as well. My favorite way to make it uses a crusty French bread that brings a satisfying crunch while remaining delicate and soft on the inside. It's topped off with a creamy seasoned butter mixture, and the key here is to use Kerrygold™ butter that will set this apart in a big way with its higher fat content that leads to a much more flavorful butter. Garlic bread can be a simple side to make, but don't let the simplicity fool you . . . it may just end up being the best bite of the entire meal.

½ cup (113 g) softened unsalted Kerrygold butter

4 cloves garlic, minced

2 tbsp (8 g) finely chopped fresh parsley

½ tsp dried oregano

½ tsp dried basil

¼ tsp salt

¼ tsp black pepper

1 loaf of French bread or baguette, cut in half lengthwise

1 cup (113 g) shredded mozzarella cheese

¼ cup (25 g) grated Parmesan cheese (optional)

Preheat the oven to 375°F (190°C).

In a small bowl, mix the butter, garlic, parsley, oregano, basil, salt and pepper. Spread the garlic butter mixture over the cut sides of the bread, making sure it's covered edge to edge. Sprinkle the shredded mozzarella cheese all over the bread, and if you want some extra flavor, go ahead and sprinkle some grated Parmesan cheese on top as well.

Place the bread on a baking sheet and into the preheated oven it goes. Bake for 12 to 15 minutes, or until the cheese turns perfectly melted and bubbly, and the edges of the bread become golden brown. Remove the garlic bread from the oven and let it cool for a few minutes before slicing it into individual servings. Make sure to do it while it's still warm, allowing the cheese to stretch and ooze.

LEMON AND DILL ROASTED CARROTS

Yield: 2–3 servings

Carrots must be one of the more common vegetables used in pretty much every household. They are affordable, accessible and bring some incredible flavor to a wide variety of recipes. Between my mom's pot roast and my grandmother's chicken and dumplings, almost all of our favorite family meals have carrots as a main ingredient. I fell in love with the flavor and texture of this vegetable, and I eventually found this tried-and-true recipe that took them from just an ingredient to the star of the show. They are rich and caramelized from the olive oil and honey base of the glaze, but with a pop of refreshing flavor that comes from the lemon and dill. This dish will have you looking at carrots in an entirely new light!

3 tbsp (45 ml) olive oil

Zest and juice of 1 lemon

½ tsp salt

1 tsp black pepper

1 tbsp (15 ml) honey

2 tsp (4 g) chopped fresh dill

1 lb (454 g) rainbow carrots

Finely grated Parmesan cheese, for topping (optional)

Preheat the oven to 400°F (204°C), and line a baking sheet with parchment paper.

In a small bowl, combine the olive oil, lemon zest, lemon juice, salt, pepper and honey. Mix everything together until smooth, and then add the dill.

To prepare the carrots, first we need to wash them. Then, hold each carrot at the stem end and carefully peel the outer layer of skin off with a peeler or paring knife. I leave the stem on, but you can remove it after peeling, if you prefer. Arrange the carrots evenly apart on the baking sheet. Brush each carrot with a generous amount of the glaze, making sure all sides are covered. Roast for 20 to 25 minutes, or until they are fork tender.

Remove the carrots from the oven, and while they are still warm, add the Parmesan (if using) over the top of the carrots. Let the carrots cool slightly before serving. Enjoy them as a side or as a delicious healthy snack!

CREAMED CORN WITH SMOKED GOUDA AND BACON

Yield: 3-4 servings

Creamed corn isn't always the first side that comes to mind when I want to add corn into the mix. I love the texture, but the flavor has always left a little to be desired for me, which is why I decided to add a smoky and salty boost of flavor to this classic corn side dish. Now this is one of my all-time favorite sides. Adding the smoked Gouda complements the already creamy nature of this dish but brings a new layer of flavor to enjoy, which is enhanced further by adding chopped bacon. This is a winner through and through, and once you give it a taste, you will never have creamed corn a different way again.

2 tbsp (28 g) unsalted butter

2 cloves garlic, minced

2 tbsp (16 g) all-purpose flour

1 cup (240 ml) milk

½ cup (120 ml) heavy cream

4 cups (640 g) frozen or fresh corn kernels

1 cup (113 g) shredded smoked Gouda cheese

½ tsp smoked paprika

Salt and pepper, to taste

4 slices bacon, cooked and crumbled

Chopped fresh parsley or green onions, for garnishing (optional)

Melt the butter in a large skillet or saucepan over medium heat, and then add the garlic and sauté until fragrant. Sprinkle the flour into the skillet and stir it into the butter and garlic to create a roux. Slowly add in the milk and heavy cream, whisking continuously to avoid any lumps. Keep stirring until the mixture thickens slightly. Stir in the corn kernels.

Reduce the heat to low and let the corn simmer until tender before adding the Gouda cheese for that incredible smoky flavor. Add the smoked paprika and stir everything together until the cheese melts. Season with salt and pepper to your taste preference.

Take the skillet off the heat and gently fold in most of the crumbled bacon, saving a little bit for a garnish. Transfer the creamy corn mixture to a serving dish and sprinkle the remaining bacon on top. For an extra touch, garnish with chopped fresh parsley.

ELOTE PASTA SALAD

Yield: 5-6 servings

I love sharing recipes that I have learned from family members and put my own twist on. My mom makes an incredible pasta salad for almost every cookout or get-together, and this is my fusion take on the recipe I learned from her many years ago. The inspiration here is one of the best street foods out there: elote. It's a staple in Mexico that combines grilled corn on the cob with creamy, spicy and salty ingredients to give you the absolute best way to enjoy corn. This dish brings everything you love about Mexican street corn and combines it with a staple side dish that everyone can enjoy in a new way.

8 oz (226 g) rotini or fusilli pasta

2 cups (340 g) cooked corn kernels (from 2-3 corncobs)

1 red bell pepper, diced

½ cup (70 g) diced red onion

½ cup (55 g) crumbled cotija cheese

¼ cup (15 g) chopped fresh cilantro, plus extra for serving

¼ cup (60 ml) mayonnaise

¼ cup (60 ml) sour cream

2 tbsp (30 ml) lime juice

1 tsp of chili powder

½ tsp of smoked paprika

½ tsp of garlic powder

Salt and pepper, to taste

Lime wedges, for serving

Cook the pasta according to the package instructions until it's al dente. Drain the pasta and rinse it under cold water to cool it down and stop the cooking process.

In a large mixing bowl, combine the cooked pasta, corn, red bell pepper, red onion, cotija cheese and cilantro. Set this aside.

In a small bowl, whisk together the mayonnaise, sour cream, lime juice, chili powder, smoked paprika, garlic powder, salt and pepper. Pour the dressing over the pasta mixture and give it a toss, being careful not to break the pasta. Grab a spoon and give it a taste, and then adjust the seasoning to your preference. Cover the bowl and pop it into the refrigerator for at least 1 hour to chill and further develop its flavor.

When you're ready to serve, give the pasta salad a gentle toss to refresh the flavors. Garnish with additional fresh cilantro and a squeeze of lime.

MISO-ROASTED SWEET POTATOES

Yield: 3–4 servings

As someone who grew up not caring for sweet potatoes, I have always looked for flavors that work well with them to create the ultimate sweet potato side that I would enjoy. The first time I tried a miso-roasted bok choy, I had the idea to bring those flavors over to this starchy side. Here, you get a balanced and bold flavor profile that works perfectly with roasted sweet potatoes, and trust me when I say that these are addicting.

2 tbsp (30 g) white miso paste

2 tbsp (30 ml) maple syrup

1 tbsp (15 ml) sesame oil

1 tbsp (15 ml) soy sauce

1 tbsp (15 ml) rice vinegar

2 large sweet potatoes, peeled and cut into cubes

1 tbsp (7 g) toasted sesame seeds

1 green onion, sliced, for garnishing

Preheat the oven to 400°F (204°C), and line a baking sheet with parchment paper.

In a small bowl, whisk together the white miso paste, maple syrup, sesame oil, soy sauce and rice vinegar until blended well. Now, it's time to coat those sweet potato cubes with all the sauce. Place the cubes in a large mixing bowl and pour the miso marinade over them. Give it a good toss to coat all the sweet potatoes with the mixture.

Transfer the coated sweet potatoes to the baking sheet, making sure to spread them out in a single layer. This way, they'll roast evenly and develop that caramelized texture we all love. Pop the baking sheet into the preheated oven and let the sweet potatoes roast for 30 to 35 minutes. Keep an eye on them, and give them a toss halfway through to make sure they cook evenly.

Once the sweet potatoes are tender and caramelized, remove them from the oven and sprinkle them with toasted sesame seeds, which add a delicious nutty flavor. Transfer the roasted sweet potatoes to a serving dish, and garnish them with the sliced green onions. This truly is the perfect combination of savory, sweet and nutty flavors in each bite.

SMOKED PAPRIKA AND CHEDDAR CORN BREAD WITH HONEY BUTTER

Yield: 6-8 servings

Cast-iron skillet corn bread is something I consider to be nearly perfect on its own. When I think about what dishes I often eat it with, it's usually something off the grill or smoker. So why not give it a nice touch of smoke itself?! This recipe is a moist and savory complement to any of your barbecue favorites, and the honey butter pairing is a match made in heaven.

For the Corn Bread

1 cup (120 g) cornmeal

1 cup (120 g) all-purpose flour

1 tbsp (15 g) baking powder

½ tsp salt

1 tsp smoked paprika

1 cup (113 g) shredded cheddar cheese

1 cup (240 ml) buttermilk

¼ cup (60 ml) melted unsalted butter

1 tbsp (15 ml) honey

2 large eggs

For the Honey Butter

½ cup (113 g) softened butter

¼ cup (60 ml) honey

Preheat the oven to 375°F (190°C), and grease a 9- to 10-inch (23- to 25-cm) cast-iron skillet.

To make the corn bread, in a large bowl, combine the cornmeal, flour, baking powder, salt and smoked paprika. Add the cheddar cheese and mix until evenly distributed. In a separate bowl, whisk together the buttermilk, butter, honey and eggs. Pour the wet ingredients into the dry ingredients, and stir gently until just combined. Be careful not to overmix the batter. Transfer the batter to the cast-iron skillet, spreading it out evenly. Place it in the preheated oven and bake for 20 to 25 minutes, or until a toothpick inserted into the center comes out clean and the top is golden brown.

While the corn bread is baking, make the honey butter. In a small bowl, combine the butter and honey, stirring until well blended. Set the honey butter aside. Once the corn bread is done, remove it from the oven and let it cool for a few minutes. Slice and serve warm with a generous dollop of delicious honey butter.

MIDDLE EASTERN CAPRESE SALAD

Yield: 4–5 servings

One of the first things my girlfriend, Amber, made for me when we started dating was a caprese salad. I always stayed away from it since I'm not a huge fan of vinegar, but the dish took me by surprise in a great way. This Middle Eastern variation of the caprese salad brings some nice flair to an already amazing dish. Juicy cherry tomatoes, creamy mozzarella pearls, fresh mint leaves and pops of sweet and tangy pomegranate arils come together perfectly with a simple dressing of extra virgin olive oil and lemon juice. Topped off with za'atar that pulls everything together, this is a refreshing complement to any meal, but goes especially well with an incredible Middle Eastern dish.

2 cups (300 g) halved cherry tomatoes

1 cup (140 g) fresh mozzarella pearls

½ cup (12 g) torn or thinly sliced fresh mint leaves

¼ cup (40 g) pomegranate arils

3 tbsp (45 ml) extra virgin olive oil

1½ tbsp (22.5 ml) lemon juice

Salt and pepper, to taste

1 tsp za'atar seasoning

Let's start with a large mixing bowl and toss in the tomatoes, mozzarella, mint, and pomegranate arils.

In a small bowl, combine the olive oil and lemon juice. Give it a good whisk, and then season with salt and pepper to your taste preference. Drizzle the dressing over the salad, and make sure to gently stir the salad, being mindful not to squish the pomegranate arils. To add a nice Middle Eastern inspired touch, sprinkle the za'atar seasoning evenly over the salad before serving.

Allow the salad to sit for a few minutes to let the flavors meld, and then you are ready to taste my favorite spin on caprese salad.

CRISPY PARMESAN BRUSSELS SPROUTS WITH LEMON AND HONEY MUSTARD SAUCE

Yield: 2-3 servings

Brussels sprouts are a love them or hate them kind of vegetable, and in my house, we LOVE them. It all comes down to the way the sprouts are prepared, and the best preparations involve ingredients that help them crisp up and develop flavor. This recipe really takes this already staple side dish to another level. These Brussels sprouts are roasted to perfection by using a seasoned oil and Parmesan mixture to create the ultimate crispy bite every time. But on top of that, we kick it up a notch by drizzling them with a tangy lemon and honey mustard sauce that makes these even more irresistible. This side dish is packed with some incredible flavors that will make you crave Brussels sprouts on a regular basis.

1 lb (454 g) Brussels sprouts, trimmed and halved

2 tbsp (30 ml) olive oil

½ cup (55 g) grated Parmesan cheese, divided

Salt and pepper, as needed

2 tbsp (30 g) Dijon mustard

1 tbsp (15 ml) honey

1 tbsp (15 ml) lemon juice

Zest of 1 lemon

Preheat the oven to 400°F (204°C), and line a baking sheet with parchment paper.

In a bowl, toss the Brussels sprouts with the olive oil, ¼ cup (27 g) of the Parmesan, salt and pepper until they are coated with the delicious mixture. Spread the remaining Parmesan on the baking sheet, and then place the Brussels, cut side down, on top of the Parmesan. Keep them spread out evenly and roast in the oven for 20 to 25 minutes, or until they are crispy and the cheese is turning golden brown.

While the Brussels sprouts are roasting, in a small bowl, whisk together the Dijon mustard, honey, lemon juice, lemon zest, salt and pepper until the ingredients are well combined. This sauce is perfect for dipping these Brussels in!

Once the Brussels sprouts are cooked, remove them from the oven and transfer them to a serving dish. Drizzle the zesty sauce over the Brussels and serve the rest for dipping.

SMALL PLATE STARTERS WITH BIG FLAVOR

There is nothing quite like a good first impression. When it comes to a good meal, appetizers have a big job in setting the tone for everything to come. I've never been a head-to-the-store-and-grab-some-snacks kind of person, especially when you can make some of the best appetizers with very little effort at home. This chapter will show you how to make some of my favorite dishes, like Caramelized Onion Chip Dip (page 88), which is the best version of a classic French onion dip that takes patience but delivers a richness and touch of smoke you won't find in any normal onion dip. We also get to have some fun with simple flavor combinations that work in a big way such as with my Cheese-Stuffed Bacon-Wrapped Dates (page 91). Each bite hits all the sweet, salty and creamy notes you expect, but also layers in some smoke that takes this appetizer to new heights. Let's dive in, and I'll show you how to make a good first impression.

THE ULTIMATE SWEET AND SPICY CHICKEN WINGS

Yield: 6–8 whole chicken wings

Chicken wings are one of the most popular appetizers out there, and that's for a good reason. They give you a blank slate to start, and whether you prefer sweet, salty, savory or spicy, you will find all of that here with these wings. These have quickly become one of my most requested appetizers because of the addictive sweet heat built into the glaze. It's the perfect complement to crispy oven-baked wings, and when I say this checks every single box on the flavor spectrum, I mean it! Modify the spice level to your preference, but I highly recommend Sriracha with this for a truly next-level appetizer.

2 lb (907 g) whole chicken wings, separated into drums and flats

2 tbsp (30 ml) olive oil

1 tsp smoked paprika

1 tsp garlic powder

1 tsp onion powder

½ tsp salt

½ tsp black pepper

¼ cup (60 ml) honey

¼ cup (60 ml) soy sauce

2 tbsp (30 ml) hot sauce, such as Sriracha or Tabasco® Pepper Sauce

1 tbsp (15 ml) rice vinegar

1 tsp grated fresh ginger

2 cloves garlic, minced

Chopped fresh cilantro, for garnishing

Toasted sesame seeds, for garnishing

Preheat the oven to 400°F (204°C), and line a baking sheet with parchment paper.

In a large bowl, toss the wings with the olive oil to coat, and then season with the paprika, garlic powder, onion powder, salt and pepper. Mix well and make sure the wings are evenly coated. Arrange the wings on the baking sheet in a single layer. Bake for 20 to 25 minutes, or until they turn golden brown and crispy.

While the wings are baking, prepare the glaze. In a small saucepan, combine the honey, soy sauce, hot sauce, rice vinegar, ginger and garlic. Heat the mixture over medium-low heat, stirring occasionally, for 15 minutes, or until it simmers and slightly thickens. After the initial baking time, remove the wings from the oven and generously brush them with the prepared glaze. Return them to the oven and bake for 7 to 10 minutes to allow the glaze to caramelize and create a sticky coating. The internal temperature should be 165 to 170°F (75 to 77°C).

Remove the wings from the oven and let them rest for a moment. Sprinkle the cilantro over the top along with the toasted sesame seeds. Make sure to have plenty of napkins on hand.

BARBECUE BACON-WRAPPED JALAPEÑO POPPERS

Yield: 5–6 servings

There is a local farm-to-table barbecue spot that my beef farmer took me to, and he insisted I try their jalapeño poppers, swearing they were like candy. I took one bite and immediately started trying to figure out what they used to make them. The blend of cheese, seasoning and crispy bacon that is finished off with barbecue sauce has quickly become one of my most requested appetizers at any get-together. The flavor combination possibilities are endless, and I highly recommend trying out different seasonings and barbecue sauces to see what you can come up with after giving these a try.

12 jalapeño peppers

8 oz (226 g) cream cheese, softened

½ cup (56 g) shredded cheddar cheese

¼ tsp garlic powder

¼ tsp onion powder

¼ tsp paprika

12 slices of uncooked bacon, cut in half

½ cup (120 ml) barbecue sauce

Preheat the oven or smoker to 325°F (163°C). This will ensure that our poppers cook to perfection. Line a baking sheet with parchment paper.

Cut off the stem end of each jalapeño pepper and slice them in half lengthwise. Take caution while handling the peppers, and make sure to remove the seeds and membranes to control the heat level.

In a small mixing bowl, combine the cream cheese, cheddar cheese, garlic powder, onion powder and paprika. Mix them together until they are well combined and creamy. Now, it's time to fill each jalapeño half with 1 tablespoon (15 g) of the cheese mixture. The creamy filling will balance out the heat of the jalapeño, creating a delicious combination of flavors. Wrap each stuffed jalapeño half with a half slice of bacon and secure it with a toothpick. Pop these in the oven or smoker for 25 to 30 minutes, or until the bacon starts to get crispy.

Brush each popper with the barbecue sauce, coating them evenly. Let them cook for 5 to 10 minutes, or until the sauce has set. Remove the poppers from the oven, and allow them to cool for a few minutes. These are my favorite when I want to indulge in the perfect balance of heat, creaminess and smoky flavors, and they are the perfect pairing to any barbecue meal.

CHARRED CORN AND BLACK BEAN QUESADILLA

Yield: 3–4 servings

Quesadillas are one of the easiest appetizers, but that doesn't mean we can't take the flavor up a notch. My son absolutely loves cheese, and quesadillas were one of the first foods he requested by name. Now I'm all for a cheese quesadilla, but I can't help incorporating some of my favorite flavors that come from spices like chili powder and cumin to bring the most out of the veggies. This makes for a great appetizer or a meal on its own, but no matter when you decide to eat it, you'll be enjoying the ultimate quesadilla.

1 corncob

½ red onion, sliced

1 red bell pepper, sliced

2 tbsp (30 ml) olive oil

Pinch of salt and black pepper, plus more to taste

1 (14-oz [400 g]) can black beans, drained and rinsed

2 cloves garlic, minced

¼ tsp cumin

¼ tsp chili powder

2 tbsp (28 g) butter

4 medium-sized tortillas

1 cup (113 g) shredded Monterey Jack cheese

¼ cup (4 g) chopped fresh cilantro

Lime wedges, for serving

Preheat your grill or grill pan over medium-high heat. This will give our veggies those beautiful, charred marks and enhance their flavors.

Brush the corn, red onion and red bell pepper with olive oil, and season with a pinch of salt and pepper. Place the vegetables on the grill and cook for 5 to 7 minutes, or until they're lightly charred and tender. Once they're done, set them aside to cool. Once the vegetables have cooled down a bit, cut the corn kernels off the cob, and chop the onion and pepper into small pieces. In a mixing bowl, combine the charred vegetables, black beans, garlic, cumin, chili powder and a bit more salt and black pepper, to taste. Give everything a good stir.

Heat a large skillet over medium heat and melt the butter. This is the key to a golden crispy quesadilla. Place one tortilla in the skillet and sprinkle ¼ cup (28 g) of the Monterey Jack cheese evenly over the tortilla. This cheese will act as the glue that holds our quesadilla together. Spoon ½ cup (85 g) of the black bean and vegetable mixture onto one side of the tortilla, spreading it evenly. This is where the flavors really start to come alive. Sprinkle 1 tablespoon of cilantro over the top of the mixture. Now, fold the tortilla in half, pressing down gently to seal it.

Cook the quesadilla for 2 to 3 minutes on each side, or until it turns crispy, and the cheese inside has melted. Repeat the process with the remaining tortillas and filling. To serve, cut the quesadillas into wedges and serve them hot. Don't forget to squeeze some fresh lime juice over the top for a pop of flavor.

PESTO BURRATA CROSTINI

Yield: 4 crostini

This is one of my favorite simple-but-flavor-packed appetizers. These are also not your average crostini. Typically, they are made with a French baguette, but we are going to need much more surface area to pack in all the flavor. Toasted crusty Italian bread is the perfect canvas to paint on some pesto and top off with creamy burrata and fresh cracked pepper. They're rich, savory, creamy and an absolute showstopper . . . and the best part is, they only take 10 minutes to make.

½ cup (120 ml) olive oil

1 tsp salt

1 tsp black pepper, plus more to taste

1 loaf of crusty Italian bread, sliced into ½" (1-cm)-thick slices (we will use 4 slices)

1 cup (240 ml) basil pesto

2 burrata cheese balls, cut in half

¼ cup (15 g) chopped fresh basil, for garnishing

Preheat the oven to 400°F (204°C). Line a baking sheet with parchment paper.

In a small bowl, whisk together the olive oil, salt and pepper. Brush this mixture over each side of the slices of bread. Place the bread slices on the baking sheet, and bake for 10 to 12 minutes, or until they turn golden brown and become crispy. Let them cool for a few minutes before spreading 1 tablespoon (15 ml) or more of the basil pesto onto each bread slice.

Top each piece of bread with a half of a creamy burrata cheese ball, followed by a little pepper. You can serve them like this or return the baking sheet to the oven and bake for another 3 to 5 minutes, or until the cheese is melted.

Remove the crostini from the oven and sprinkle with freshly chopped basil. Cut them diagonally, serve warm and watch them disappear within seconds.

CRAFT BEER-BATTERED ONION RINGS WITH CHIPOTLE AIOLI

Yield: 2–3 servings

These onion rings are the perfect combination of crispy, golden-brown goodness and a smoky, tangy dipping sauce. The secret ingredient? A great craft beer. The batter infused with the rich flavors of beer creates an irresistible crunch that pairs perfectly with the zesty chipotle aioli. It's a simple dish with a depth of flavor that is hard to top.

For the Onion Rings

1½ cups (180 g) all-purpose flour

½ cup (60 g) panko breadcrumbs

2 tsp (4 g) garlic powder

2 tsp (4 g) smoked paprika

1 tsp cayenne pepper

1 tsp salt

½ tsp black pepper

1½ cups (360 ml) craft beer (preferably a lager or ale)

Vegetable oil, for frying

2 large yellow onions, cut into ½" (1-cm)-thick rings

For the Chipotle Aioli

½ cup (120 ml) mayonnaise

1 tbsp (15 ml) adobo sauce (from a can of chipotle peppers in adobo)

1 tbsp (15 ml) fresh lime juice

1 clove garlic, minced

Salt and black pepper, to taste

In a large mixing bowl, combine the flour, breadcrumbs, garlic powder, paprika, cayenne pepper, salt and pepper. Now it's time to add the star ingredient: craft beer. Slowly pour in the beer while whisking constantly until a smooth batter forms.

Heat the vegetable oil in a large, heavy-bottomed pot or deep fryer to 375°F (190°C). We want the oil to be hot enough to create that perfect crispy texture. Dip an onion ring into the batter, making sure it's well coated. Carefully place it into the hot oil, and you'll hear that sizzling sound. Repeat this step with the remaining onion rings, frying them in batches.

As the onion rings fry, they'll turn a beautiful golden brown and become irresistibly crispy. Keep an eye on them, and flip them occasionally for even cooking. It should take 2 to 3 minutes per batch. Once the onion rings are perfectly fried, use a slotted spoon or tongs to transfer them to a paper towel–lined plate. This will help remove any excess oil and keep the onion rings light and crispy.

While the onion rings cool slightly, prepare the chipotle aioli. In a small bowl, mix the mayonnaise, adobo sauce, lime juice, garlic, salt and pepper. This creamy and smoky sauce is the perfect match for our crispy onion rings.

CARAMELIZED ONION CHIP DIP

Yield: 4–6 servings

French onion chip dip is one of those nostalgic appetizers that takes me back to cookouts at my grandparents' as a kid. I would usually just buy my chip dip over the years instead of trying to make it on my own, but after tasting the difference in homemade dip a few years ago, I never went back. This is a twist on one of the most iconic dips and is elevated by adding the richness of caramelized onions and a touch of smoky flavor. Make this ahead and let the flavors really develop overnight.

2 tbsp (28 g) butter

1 tbsp (15 ml) olive oil

2 large onions, thinly sliced

1 tsp salt

½ tsp black pepper

½ cup (120 ml) mayonnaise

½ cup (120 ml) sour cream

¼ tsp garlic powder

¼ tsp onion powder

¼ tsp smoked paprika

¼ tsp Worcestershire sauce

1 tbsp (3 g) chopped fresh chives, for garnishing

In a large skillet, melt the butter with the olive oil over medium-low to medium heat. Add the onions and season with salt and pepper. Cook the onions, stirring occasionally, for 40 to 45 minutes, or until they become caramelized and turn a golden-brown color. True caramelized onions take time, so don't rush this step. Remove the skillet from the heat and allow the onions to cool for 10 to 15 minutes. Dice the onions to give the dip a better texture, and set aside.

In a medium bowl, mix together the mayonnaise, sour cream, garlic powder, onion powder, smoked paprika and Worcestershire sauce. Add the onions to the mayonnaise mixture and stir until well combined. Transfer the dip to a serving bowl and garnish with the chives. Serve this delicious dip with your favorite chips or vegetables, and get ready to enjoy your new staple dip for any game day, cookout or get-together.

CHEESE-STUFFED BACON-WRAPPED DATES

Yield: 2–3 servings

You might be skeptical if I told you that this is one of the best things I've ever made. But the sweet, savory, salty combo makes this bite of food one of the most addicting things to ever come out of my oven (these can be made in the smoker as well by following the same instructions). What sets these apart from others is the way we incorporate the perfect amount of spice and additional flavor into the cheese filling, which is often left plain. If you want to surprise everyone with a bite-sized creamy and smoky treat that they will absolutely love, give these a shot. Just make sure you stash a few for yourself because these quickly disappear.

4 oz (113 g) goat cheese

4 oz (113 g) cream cheese

1 tsp crushed red chili flakes

½ tsp smoked paprika

24 Medjool dates

12 slices of bacon, cut in half

Preheat the oven to 375°F (190°C).

In a small mixing bowl, combine the goat cheese, cream cheese, crushed red chili flakes and smoked paprika. Give them a good stir until they're well combined and smooth.

Slice each Medjool date lengthwise, removing the pit carefully. This will create a pocket for our cheese filling. Stuff each date with ½ teaspoon of the cheese mixture. The combination of goat cheese and cream cheese adds a tangy and rich flavor to the sweet dates. Wrap each stuffed date with a half slice of bacon. Secure each with a toothpick.

Arrange the dates on a baking sheet, making sure to space them apart for even cooking. Bake for 15 to 20 minutes, or until the bacon turns crispy and the cheese melts. Allow these to cool for a few minutes before serving.

SPICY CRAB RANGOON DIP

Yield: 4-6 servings

It's very rare that I don't get myself some crab rangoon when I order Chinese food. The creamy, fried, wonton-wrapped appetizer just screams comfort food, and this dip is my way of putting my own spin on it. The best part of crab rangoon is the delicious lump crabmeat and the balance of creamy and tangy flavors that make up the filling. So, why not make these the star of the show? This dip gives you full control over how much filling you get with each bite, and you never have to worry about the wontons getting soggy. Serve with crispy wonton chips or crackers, and start your meal off with a bang.

8 oz (226 g) cream cheese, softened

½ cup (120 ml) sour cream

½ cup (120 ml) mayonnaise

1 cup (225 g) drained lump crabmeat

½ cup (32 g) finely chopped green onions

¼ cup (60 ml) hot sauce (such as Sriracha), plus extra for serving

1 tsp garlic powder

1 tsp onion powder

1 tsp soy sauce

Salt and pepper, as needed

Wonton chips or crackers, for serving

Preheat the oven to 350°F (175°C).

In a large bowl, combine the cream cheese, sour cream and mayonnaise. Stir until the mixture is smooth and well combined. Add the crabmeat and green onions. Gently stir to evenly distribute the ingredients throughout the creamy base. Add the hot sauce, garlic powder, onion powder, soy sauce, salt and pepper. Stir well to ensure the mixture is properly seasoned and all the flavors are incorporated.

Transfer the dip to an oven-safe baking dish, smoothing the top with a spatula for an even finish. Bake for 20 to 25 minutes, or until it becomes hot and bubbly. Allow the dip to cool for a few minutes before serving. I prefer to eat this with crispy wonton chips, but you can also use your favorite crackers.

SAVORY THYME FRENCH ONION SOUP

Yield: 8 servings

If I had to eat soup every day, it would be this one, no questions asked. When I got my first job at a local restaurant, they were known for having the best French onion soup around, and I always wanted to learn how to make it. I could never convince the owner to share the recipe, but I'd like to think I got pretty darn close with this one, and of course I added a bit of my own spin on it. The addition of smoked paprika brings a delicious earthiness that complements the fresh thyme and Worcestershire sauce extremely well. This is a soup you must plan ahead for since it does take some time, but you will not regret it one bit.

2 tbsp (28 g) butter

2 tbsp (30 ml) olive oil

6 large yellow onions, thinly sliced

½ cup (120 ml) dry white wine

6 cups (1.4 L) beef or chicken broth

2 cups (480 ml) water

2 bay leaves

2 tbsp (30 ml) Worcestershire sauce

4 sprigs of fresh thyme

1 tsp smoked paprika

Salt and black pepper, as needed

1 French baguette, cut into ¼–½" (6-mm–1-cm)-thick slices

2 cups (200 g) shredded Gruyère cheese

Fresh parsley, chopped, for garnishing

In a large pot or Dutch oven, melt the butter and olive oil over medium heat. Add the onions and stir to coat them. Cook, stirring occasionally, for 40 to 50 minutes, or until the onions are deeply caramelized and tender. Pour in the white wine and stir to scrape up any browned bits from the bottom of the pot, adding extra flavor to the soup. Add the broth, water, bay leaves, Worcestershire sauce, thyme, paprika, salt and pepper to the pot. Stir well to combine all the ingredients and bring the soup to a gentle simmer. Allow the soup to simmer for 30 to 40 minutes, giving the flavors time to meld together and develop a rich and aromatic base.

Preheat the oven to 375°F (190°C).

Arrange the baguette slices on a baking sheet and toast them in the oven until they turn lightly golden.

Remove the bay leaves from the soup and ladle the flavorful soup into oven-safe bowls. Top each bowl with a few slices of toasted baguette and generously sprinkle shredded Gruyère cheese over the top of the bread.

Preheat the oven to high broil.

Place the bowls under the broiler in the oven for 3 to 5 minutes, or until the cheese is melted and beautifully bubbly. Garnish each bowl with a sprinkle of the parsley, adding a touch of freshness and color. Serve piping hot and savor each spoonful of the rich and comforting flavors.

GRILLED FLATBREAD WITH WHIPPED FETA AND ROASTED VEGETABLES

Yield: 1–2 servings

One of my favorite shareable appetizers that I can always get creative with is grilled flatbread. All you'll need to make what I consider the best flatbread out there is a grill, a whisk or electric mixer and a mixing bowl. It's the perfect refreshing bite of Mediterranean flavors. This is just one of those appetizers that you have to make plenty of because the whole family will devour these.

½ cup (70 g) crumbled feta cheese

¼ cup (60 ml) plain Greek yogurt

2 tbsp (30 ml) fresh lemon juice

2 cloves garlic, minced

¼ cup (60 ml) extra virgin olive oil, plus more as needed

Salt and black pepper, as needed

1 small red onion, sliced

1 red bell pepper, sliced

1 small zucchini, sliced

1 small eggplant, sliced

2 tbsp (8 g) chopped fresh oregano

1 tbsp (4 g) chopped fresh thyme

2 large prepackaged flatbreads

1 tbsp (3 g) chopped fresh parsley, for garnishing

In a medium bowl, combine the feta, yogurt, lemon juice, garlic and a drizzle of the olive oil. Season with salt and pepper. Give it a good mix until you have a smooth and creamy consistency, and then set aside. In a large bowl, add the onion, bell pepper, zucchini, eggplant, ¼ cup (60 ml) of the olive oil, salt, pepper, oregano and thyme. Toss until the veggies are coated evenly with the oil and seasoning.

Fire up the grill to medium-high heat. While the grill is heating, brush both sides of the flatbreads with olive oil. Place the flatbread on the grill and let them cook for a few minutes on each side until they develop a beautiful char and turn crispy. Once the flatbreads are done grilling, it's time to grill our seasoned vegetables. Lay the sliced vegetables on a metal cooling rack and place this directly on the grill. Cook them for 3 to 4 minutes or until tender and slightly charred.

When the flatbreads and vegetables are cooked to perfection, it's time to assemble our flatbread. Spread the whipped feta mixture generously over each grilled flatbread. Then, layer on the grilled vegetables, creating a colorful and mouthwatering feast for the eyes. To savor the flavors at their best, slice the flatbread into wedges and top with the parsley. Whether you're enjoying this grilled flatbread as an appetizer or a meal, prepare yourself for an unforgettable medley of flavors.

SMOKED SALMON DIP

Yield: 6–8 servings

Initially, I wasn't a huge fan of smoked salmon. But during a recent trip to Mississippi, I tried a smoked salmon dip that blew me away, and I didn't have a recipe, but I had to give it a shot. Through trial and error, I landed on a version with charred smoked salmon and fresh dill that was simple but unforgettable. The secret here is using a culinary torch or open flame to slightly char the salmon, which adds a ton of depth to a classic dip. Whether it's for a cookout, potluck or family dinner, give this a shot. It'll be the standout dish.

4 oz (113 g) smoked salmon

1 tsp olive oil

8 oz (226 g) cream cheese, softened

¼ cup (60 ml) sour cream

¼ cup (60 ml) mayonnaise

1 tbsp (15 ml) lemon juice

½ tsp garlic powder

½ tsp onion powder

½ tsp fresh dill

¼ tsp salt

¼ tsp black pepper

1 tbsp (15 ml) chopped fresh chives, for garnishing

Assorted crackers, chips or sliced vegetables, for serving

Lightly coat the salmon with the olive oil, and using either a culinary torch or directly over an open flame, give the salmon a light char on the outside, which should only take 45 to 60 seconds. Set the salmon aside to cool slightly before chopping it into small pieces.

In a large bowl, combine the cream cheese, sour cream and mayonnaise, and mix until smooth and creamy. Add the lemon juice, garlic powder, onion powder, dill, salt and pepper. Stir until all the ingredients are thoroughly combined. Gently fold in the salmon, ensuring it is evenly distributed throughout the dip. Transfer the dip to a serving bowl and garnish with chopped fresh chives for an extra pop of flavor and color.

For the flavors to meld together, refrigerate the dip for at least 30 minutes before serving. This will allow the dip to chill and elevate the taste even more. Serve with an assortment of crackers, chips or sliced vegetables.

RISE AND DINE

Breakfast may not be considered the most important meal of the day anymore, but it's still one of my favorites. I love how fusion dishes as well as elevated recipes work so well for breakfast, and I can't think of a better way to kick off the day than by enjoying one of these incredible recipes. This chapter has one of my favorite creations, Chorizo Gravy and Biscuits (page 103), which I found through my love of experimenting with different flavors. This chapter also has some options that really bring the heat in a few ways, like the Kimchi Breakfast Tacos (page 116) and the Honey Pepper Chicken and Waffles (page 108). Let's get started and prepare some amazing meals to kick off your day.

CHORIZO GRAVY AND BISCUITS

Yield: 8–10 biscuits

Sausage gravy and biscuits were a staple of my childhood, and I still consider them to be one of the all-time greatest comfort foods. As I have grown to really enjoy some of the unique variations or sausages out there, I've gravitated toward chorizo as my absolute favorite. This dish brings all the spice and flavor of chorizo and pairs it with the welcoming and warm dish we all know and love.

For the Biscuits

6 tbsp (85 g) unsalted butter, plus melted butter for brushing

2 cups (250 g) all-purpose flour, plus extra as needed

1 tbsp (15 g) baking powder

1 tbsp (12 g) sugar

1 tsp salt

¼ tsp baking soda

1 cup (240 ml) buttermilk

For the Gravy

2 tbsp (28 g) unsalted butter

1½ lb (680 g) pork chorizo

3 tbsp (23 g) all-purpose flour

2 cups (480 ml) whole milk

1 tsp black pepper, plus more to taste

1–2 tbsp (9–18 g) cotija cheese

1 tbsp (2 g) cilantro

Preheat the oven to 450°F (232°C). Line a baking sheet with a silicone mat.

To make the dough, cut the butter into cubes and place in the freezer to chill for 5 minutes. To a large food processor add the flour, baking powder, sugar, salt and baking soda. Pulse until everything is mixed well. Add the butter from the freezer to the food processor, and pulse until the butter crumbles and the mixture has a coarse consistency. Transfer the mixture to a large bowl and add the buttermilk, mixing it in until the dough becomes tacky. You can add additional flour, 1 tablespoon (8 g) at a time until the consistency is right.

Place the dough on a floured surface, and roll it out into an 8-inch (20-cm)-long rectangle. Fold the dough into thirds and roll it out again, repeating the process two more times. Once you are done, you need to roll the dough out one last time until it is 1 inch (2.5 cm) thick. Use a 2½- to 3-inch (6- to 8-cm) biscuit cutter and place the biscuits on the baking sheet. The biscuits should be close but not touching. Bake for 12 to 14 minutes, or until they are golden brown.

While the biscuits bake, make the gravy. Melt the butter in a skillet over a medium heat. Once the butter starts to brown, add the chorizo and break it down with a wooden spoon or spatula. You want to make sure the chorizo is fully cooked before moving to the next step. This should take 5 to 8 minutes. Sprinkle the flour over the top of the chorizo and stir it in while continuing to cook the mixture for 20 to 45 seconds. By now a fragrant roux should start to form, and you can add the milk to the pan. It's important to keep stirring at this stage while the gravy starts to thicken. When you reach the desired consistency, season with pepper, and stir for 20 to 30 seconds before setting the gravy aside.

Remove the biscuits from the oven and brush them with melted butter. The biscuits need to cool slightly before you can split them in half. Pour a generous amount of the chorizo gravy over the top of the biscuits. Lastly, finish them off with a small amount of cotija cheese and some cilantro. You are now ready to enjoy.

IRRESISTIBLE FRENCH TOAST WITH FRESH BERRY COMPOTE AND TOASTED ALMONDS

Yield: 3–4 servings

French toast can be as simple or as complex to make as you want it to be. One of the things I love most about cooking is finding new ways to take a simple dish and pack as much flavor into every bite as possible. This dish takes three different kinds of fresh berries that already work well with French toast and creates a warm and decadent sauce known as a compote. It's similar to a jelly or jam but has a freshness to it that you just can't find in a bottle or jar. Topped off with toasted sliced almonds, this breakfast has layers of texture and looks just as amazing as it tastes. It's a breakfast or brunch standout that has earned its reputation as the best version of French toast I've ever had.

For the French Toast

4 large eggs

½ cup (120 ml) milk

2 tbsp (25 g) granulated sugar

1 tsp vanilla extract

¼ tsp ground cinnamon

⅛ tsp salt

8 slices of thick-cut brioche bread

1 tbsp (14 g) unsalted butter, plus more as needed

For the Compote

2 cups (300 g) 3 different types of fresh mixed berries (such as strawberries, raspberries and blueberries)

¼ cup (50 g) granulated sugar

1 tbsp (15 ml) fresh lemon juice

¼ tsp vanilla extract

¼ cup (28 g) sliced almonds, for serving

To make the French toast, in a shallow bowl, whisk together the eggs, milk, sugar, vanilla extract, cinnamon and salt until they come together to form a custard. Dip each slice of bread into the egg mixture, ensuring that both sides are fully coated. Heat a large nonstick skillet or griddle over medium heat, and melt the butter. Cook each slice for 2 to 3 minutes on each side. We're aiming for a beautiful golden-brown color. Feel free to add more butter to the skillet as needed.

While our French toast is cooking, make the berry compote. In a small saucepan, combine the berries, sugar, lemon juice and vanilla extract. Cook everything over medium heat, stirring occasionally, for 10 minutes, or until the berries soften and the mixture transforms into a thick, tasty compote.

Grab a separate small skillet and toast the sliced almonds over medium heat until they turn a gorgeous golden brown and release an irresistible fragrance. This process usually takes 3 to 4 minutes, so keep an eye on them to avoid any burning mishaps. Serve the warm French toast, placing a generous dollop of the berry compote on top. Then, sprinkle the toasted almonds over the creation, adding a delightful crunch that takes this dish to the next level.

APPLE CINNAMON PANCAKES WITH BOURBON CARAMEL

Yield: 2-3 servings

I'm a bourbon guy, and if you give me the opportunity to find ways to cook with it, I will always take you up on it. This was the first time I was able to find a way to incorporate bourbon into a breakfast dish, and the bourbon caramel is a perfect finishing touch on these apple cinnamon pancakes. Most of the bourbon on the market naturally has delicious notes of vanilla, caramel and stone fruit, and the caramel sauce lets those flavors shine through in a big way while not taking away from the amazing pancakes. If you are craving something on the sweeter side for breakfast, you won't find anything better than this dish.

For the Bourbon Caramel Sauce

1 cup (200 g) granulated sugar

¼ cup (60 ml) water

½ cup (120 ml) heavy cream

2 tbsp (28 g) unsalted butter

1 tbsp (15 ml) bourbon

¼ tsp salt

For the Apple Cinnamon Pancakes

1 cup (120 g) all-purpose flour

2 tbsp (25 g) granulated sugar

2 tsp (10 g) baking powder

¼ tsp baking soda

¼ tsp salt

1 tsp ground cinnamon

1 cup (240 ml) milk

1 large egg

2 tbsp (30 ml) melted unsalted butter

1 medium apple, peeled and grated

To make the bourbon caramel sauce, in a medium saucepan, combine the sugar and water. Cook over medium-high heat, stirring occasionally until the sugar has dissolved and the mixture comes to a boil. Stop stirring and watch as it transforms into a deep amber color, which usually takes 6 to 8 minutes. Remove from the heat and carefully whisk in the heavy cream, butter, bourbon and salt. Be cautious as the mixture will bubble up.

To make the pancakes, in a medium bowl, whisk together the flour, sugar, baking powder, baking soda, salt and cinnamon. This combination of ingredients will be the secret to fluffy and flavorful pancakes. In a separate bowl, whisk together the milk, egg and melted butter until they come together in a smooth mixture. Add the wet ingredients to the dry ingredients and stir until they come together—be careful not to overmix. We want a batter that's just combined, ensuring tender pancakes. Fold in the apple.

Grease a large nonstick skillet or griddle and heat over medium heat. Use a ¼-cup (60-ml) measuring cup to pour the pancake batter onto the skillet. Watch as bubbles form on the surface and the bottom turns a golden brown, which takes 2 to 3 minutes. Flip the pancakes and cook the other side for an additional 1 to 2 minutes, or until it reaches that perfect golden color, and then set aside.

Serve the warm, fluffy pancakes with a generous drizzle of the bourbon caramel sauce. Enjoy these for a sweet and indulgent breakfast or brunch experience.

HONEY PEPPER CHICKEN AND WAFFLES

Yield: 3-4 servings

About nine years ago, I came across honey pepper fried chicken at a local restaurant, and it blew my mind how well the flavors worked together. I worked on a few copycat recipes to try to figure it out and eventually came up with this version when I was looking to put a spicy twist on chicken and waffles. The honey sauce has an addicting kick and takes an already amazing flavor combination to new levels with this dish.

For the Waffles

1½ cups (180 g) all-purpose flour

1 tbsp (15 g) baking powder

1 tbsp (15 g) granulated sugar

½ tsp salt

1¼ cups (300 ml) milk

¼ cup (60 ml) vegetable oil

2 large eggs

½ tsp vanilla extract

For the Honey Pepper Chicken

½ cup (60 g) all-purpose flour

2 tsp (8 g) garlic powder

2 tsp (8 g) onion powder

1 tsp paprika

½ tsp salt

½ tsp black pepper

6-8 chicken breasts

¾ cup (180 ml) honey

¼ cup (50 g) brown sugar

¼ cup (60 ml) pineapple juice

3 tbsp (45 ml) soy sauce

Juice of 1 lemon

¼ cup (60 ml) apple cider vinegar

1 tsp black pepper, plus more to taste

¼ tsp cayenne pepper

Vegetable oil, for frying

Preheat your waffle iron according to the manufacturer's instructions.

To make the waffles, in a large bowl, combine the flour, baking powder, sugar and salt. In a separate bowl, whisk together the milk, vegetable oil, eggs and vanilla extract. Gently add the wet ingredients to the dry mixture until just combined. Cook the waffles to the manufacturer's instructions, typically adding ½ cup (120 ml) of batter or more at a time depending on the size of the waffle iron. Set each waffle on a cooling rack to prevent them from getting soggy.

Now, let's make the Honey Pepper Chicken. In a shallow dish, combine the flour, garlic powder, onion powder, paprika, salt and pepper. Dredge each chicken breast in the flour mixture, ensuring they are evenly coated, and then set aside. In a small bowl, whisk together the honey, brown sugar, pineapple juice, soy sauce, lemon juice, apple cider vinegar, pepper and cayenne pepper. Set this aside while we start to cook the chicken.

Preheat a large skillet over medium-high heat with 1 inch (2.5 cm) of oil. Place the coated chicken in the preheated skillet and cook for 4 to 5 minutes per side, or until golden brown and cooked through. Once you remove the chicken from the skillet, generously brush the honey pepper sauce onto each piece to get a perfect glaze. Place the savory honey pepper chicken on top of the fluffy waffles. If desired, drizzle with additional sauce for an extra kick of flavor.

ZA'ATAR AND FETA BREAKFAST PITA

Yield: 4 breakfast pitas

Being half Middle Eastern, I've grown to really appreciate the bold flavors used in the dishes from all over that region of the world. One of my favorite snacks is Jordanian za'atar, which is served as a dip alongside olive oil and pita bread. It has such a unique flavor profile. This breakfast dish combines what I love about za'atar and other Middle Eastern flavors with eggs to create the ultimate handheld meal to start your day.

2 large pitas

8 large eggs

½ cup (70 g) crumbled feta cheese

Pinch of salt and pepper

2 tbsp (30 ml) olive oil

1 tbsp (8 g) za'atar spice blend

Chopped fresh parsley or mint

Diced tomatoes, sliced cucumbers and/or avocado, for serving (optional)

Preheat the oven to 350°F (175°C).

Cut the pitas in half, and toast them in the oven for 1 to 2 minutes, or until they turn slightly crispy. Set aside.

In a small bowl, whisk together the eggs and feta. Add a pinch of salt and pepper to season the mixture. Heat the olive oil in a nonstick skillet over medium heat. Pour in the egg and feta mixture and scramble until the eggs are fully cooked and fluffy. The key is to keep stirring while you scramble to avoid the eggs getting too hot. In another small bowl, combine the za'atar spice blend with a pinch of salt, creating our finishing seasoning.

It's time to assemble our breakfast pita. Generously fill each pita half with the scrambled eggs and feta cheese mixture. Sprinkle the za'atar spice blend over the eggs. Finish it up by garnishing with some chopped parsley. If you feel like taking it one step further, consider adding diced tomatoes, sliced cucumbers or creamy avocado to elevate the flavors more and boost the nutritional value.

SHAKSHUKA BENEDICT

Yield: 2 servings

As someone who isn't a big fan of hollandaise sauce, I have always looked for different ways to make the ever-popular eggs Benedict. With the perfect pairing of eggs and shakshuka sauce, this fusion take on a classic breakfast was a no-brainer. This is one of the absolute best versions of eggs Benedict, and it's a very approachable savory recipe that I promise will make its way into your breakfast rotation once you give it a shot.

4 large eggs

2 tbsp (30 ml) olive oil

1 onion, chopped

2 cloves garlic, minced

1 red bell pepper, chopped

1 (14½-oz [411-g]) can diced tomatoes, drained

1 tbsp (15 g) tomato paste

1 tsp ground cumin

½ tsp smoked paprika

Salt and black pepper, as needed

2 English muffins, split

½ cup (70 g) crumbled feta cheese

2 tbsp (8 g) chopped fresh parsley leaves

Let's start by poaching the eggs. Bring a pot of water to a gentle boil. Crack one of the eggs into a small bowl. Using a spoon, stir the water in one direction to create a whirlpool. Carefully drop the egg into the center of the whirlpool and let it cook for 3 to 4 minutes, or until the whites are set but the yolk is still delightfully runny. Use a slotted spoon to remove the poached egg from the water and set it aside. Repeat this process for the remaining eggs. Don't be worried if it takes a few attempts to get right; practice makes perfect with this technique.

In a large skillet over medium-high heat, heat the olive oil. Add the onion and garlic, and sauté for 3 minutes, or until they become soft and fragrant. Add the bell pepper and cook for 2 minutes, or until it slightly softens. Stir in the diced tomatoes, tomato paste, cumin, smoked paprika and season with salt and pepper. Allow the mixture to simmer for 10 to 12 minutes, or until it thickens.

While the shakshuka sauce is simmering, toast the English muffins and get them ready to serve. To assemble the Shakshuka Benedict, place a toasted English muffin half on each plate. Top each with a poached egg, and generously spoon the luscious shakshuka sauce over the egg. Sprinkle the dish with crumbled feta cheese and a sprinkle of freshly chopped parsley. Serve your Shakshuka Benedict immediately and savor the incredible blend of flavors. Enjoy the runny yolk, the rich shakshuka sauce and the delightful tang of feta cheese. It's a one-of-a-kind breakfast experience.

ITALIAN FRITTATA

Yield: 4–5 servings

Italian food is always at the top of my list of favorite cuisines. How can you not love a dish that has found a way to use Parmesan, basil, sun-dried tomatoes and much more all in one? This was the first frittata I ever made, and I use this as the base for most of them that I make nowadays. Feel free to get creative with your frittata by adding cooked Italian sausage, prosciutto or diced pancetta to the vegetable mixture. Experiment with different herbs and spices like oregano, thyme or red pepper flakes to customize the flavor according to your taste.

8 large eggs

¼ cup (60 ml) milk

¼ cup (25 g) grated Parmesan cheese

¼ cup (15 g) chopped fresh basil

¼ cup (15 g) chopped fresh parsley

½ tsp salt

¼ tsp black pepper

2 tbsp (30 ml) olive oil

¼ cup (40 g) chopped sun-dried tomatoes

½ cup (60 g) sliced mushrooms

½ cup (80 g) diced red bell pepper

½ cup (80 g) diced yellow onion

2 cloves garlic, minced

Italian sausage, prosciutto or diced pancetta (optional)

Oregano, thyme or crushed red pepper flakes (optional)

Preheat the oven to 375°F (190°C).

In a large bowl, whisk together the eggs, milk, Parmesan, basil, parsley, salt and pepper.

Heat the olive oil in a large oven-safe skillet over medium-high heat. Add the sun-dried tomatoes, mushrooms, bell pepper, onion and garlic. Cook for 5 minutes, or until the vegetables become tender and aromatic. Pour the egg mixture over the vegetables. Gently stir everything together to distribute the ingredients evenly throughout the frittata. Cook for 5 minutes. You'll notice that the edges will start to set, and the bottom will develop a beautiful golden-brown color. Transfer the skillet to the oven and bake for 10 to 12 minutes. Keep an eye on it and look for the top to become set and lightly golden brown. This will ensure a moist and fluffy frittata.

Once the frittata is ready, take it out of the oven and let it cool for a few minutes before slicing and serving. This allows the flavors to settle and makes it easier to handle.

KIMCHI BREAKFAST TACOS

Yield: 6 tacos

These tacos will absolutely get your day started off with a bang. They are a delicious twist on traditional breakfast tacos using a very bold ingredient: kimchi. Pairing the zing of kimchi with fluffy scrambled eggs and melted cheddar cheese, all packed into a toasted tortilla, will definitely add some excitement to your breakfast routine.

6 small flour tortillas

2 tbsp (30 ml) vegetable oil

1 cup (220 g) drained and chopped kimchi

6 large eggs

½ cup (56 g) grated Cheddar cheese

Salt and black pepper, to taste

Fresh cilantro and queso fresco, for garnishing

Heat the tortillas in a dry skillet over medium heat. Flip them after 20 to 30 seconds on each side, or until they're warm and slightly charred. Keep them warm by covering them with a clean towel. In a separate skillet, heat the vegetable oil over medium-high heat. Add the kimchi and sauté for 2 to 3 minutes, or until it becomes slightly crispy. Crack the eggs into the skillet, and gently stir until they become scrambled and cooked to your preferred level of doneness. Sprinkle the Cheddar over the mixture. Continue stirring gently until the cheese melts into the eggs. Season to taste with salt and pepper.

Divide the flavorful mixture evenly among the warm tortillas. To add a touch of freshness, top your tacos with fresh cilantro leaves and queso fresco. Enjoy one of my favorite unique breakfast experiences and let the bold flavors of kimchi awaken your senses. These tacos are sure to become a new favorite in your house.

THE BEST OATS YOU'LL EVER EAT—TIRAMISU OATS

Yield: 1 serving

When I know I'm going to have a hectic morning, I love to make overnight oats for a quick meal on the go to save some time the next day. It's incredibly easy to make, and you have an endless supply of options when it comes to flavors. Since I am a coffee lover to the highest degree, I tend to gravitate toward this incredible version of tiramisu oats. It's filling and gives me that extra kick of energy I always need to start my day. I am a huge fan of experiments in the kitchen and testing out new flavors, but this has become just about the only oats I will eat nowadays.

½ cup (40 g) old-fashioned rolled oats

⅔ cup (160 ml) cashew milk, or any milk of choice

1 tsp instant coffee

1 tbsp (15 ml) honey

¼ tsp vanilla extract

⅛ tsp salt

½ tsp cinnamon

1 tsp chia seeds

¼ cup (60 ml) Greek yogurt

Cocoa powder, for serving

Espresso beans, for serving

In a small bowl, combine the oats, milk, coffee, honey, vanilla extract, salt, cinnamon, chia and yogurt. Stir until everything is evenly spread throughout. Transfer the oat mixture to a Mason jar or other container with a lid. Place the lid on the container, give the container a good shake and pop it in the fridge for at least 8 hours.

When you're ready to eat it, take the lid off and dust half of the top with cocoa powder, garnish with a few espresso beans and enjoy a simple and delicious breakfast on the go.

BITE . . . INDULGE A LITTLE

Let's face it, we all have a sweet tooth, and sometimes it's hard to satisfy. Both my son and girlfriend have a real bias here and would probably say this chapter is the most important one to include in the book. Baking, at its core, is the best canvas for tying unique and new flavors together into a rich, sweet and satisfying treat. A must try is the Baklava Bread Pudding (page 123) that is a completely new spin on a very comforting dish. Or you can spice it up with the Bourbon Chocolate Pecan Pie with Salted Caramel Drizzle (page 131), which is my favorite by far. No matter what recipe you try, you can't go wrong.

BAKLAVA BREAD PUDDING

Yield: 6-8 servings

If you're a fan of Middle Eastern desserts, you know there's nothing quite like the rich, nutty and sweet flavors of baklava. But have you ever thought about turning the classic treat into the ultimate bread pudding? Combining the fluffy dough, honey and mixed nuts with the comforting texture and custardy richness of bread pudding makes this dessert a true masterpiece. Whether you're a fan of Middle Eastern desserts or simply looking to try something new and delicious, this bread pudding is sure to satisfy your sweet cravings.

6-7 cups (720-840 g) cubed challah or brioche bread

For the Baklava Mixture

1 cup (120 g) pistachios

1 cup (120 g) walnuts

¼ cup (50 g) light brown sugar

1 tsp ground cinnamon

For the Custard

3 cups (710 ml) whole milk

½ cup (120 ml) heavy cream

¼ cup (50 g) light brown sugar

4 large eggs

1 tbsp (15 ml) vanilla extract

½ tsp ground cinnamon

Honey, for serving

Place the bread cubes on a cooling rack to dry out slightly while you prepare the rest of the ingredients.

To make the baklava mixture, in a food processor, add the pistachios, walnuts, sugar and cinnamon, and then process on low for 30 seconds. Continue to pulse the mixture until the desired consistency is achieved—you are looking for small, chopped pieces. Set this aside.

To make the custard, in a large bowl, add the milk, heavy cream, sugar, eggs, vanilla extract and ground cinnamon. Whisk to mix and bring everything together in a nice smooth consistency. Be careful not to overmix the ingredients—once you have achieved a smooth and creamy custard, we are all set.

Grease a 12 x 8-inch (30 x 20-cm) or 13 x 9-inch (33 x 23-cm) baking dish. Place the bread cubes in the dish, making sure they're evenly spread throughout before sprinkling the baklava mixture over the top of the bread. To get the best result, I like to make sure some of that baklava mixture also gets in between the pieces of bread. Then pour the custard evenly over the bread. It's very important to make sure all the pieces are coated. Cover the baking dish with foil and place it in the fridge for at least 4 hours, or up to 8 hours.

Preheat the oven to 350°F (175°C) degrees.

Remove the bread pudding from the fridge and place it directly in the oven with the foil still in place. Bake for 18 to 20 minutes, and then remove the foil. Bake for 25 minutes, or until the top is golden brown. Let it cool slightly, and then serve warm with a drizzle of honey.

PUMPKIN CHEESECAKE

Yield: 8–10 servings

If you're a fan of all those pumpkin flavors that come around every fall, get ready for the best version of pumpkin cheesecake you'll ever taste. The real difference maker is using pasture-raised eggs from companies like The Happy Egg Company® that have a much richer yolk; this gives the cheesecake unmatched flavor and a silky-smooth texture. Pairing it with freshly ground aromatic spices sets this cheesecake apart from the rest without overcomplicating it. Pumpkin desserts like this check the nostalgia box for me in a big way. I was born on Thanksgiving, and having pumpkin pie on my birthday instead of a cake became a pretty regular occurrence—and if it wasn't that, it was pumpkin cheesecake. This dessert screams the holidays, but it's an amazing treat any time of the year.

For the Crust

1½ cups (150 g) graham cracker crumbs

¼ cup (60 ml) melted butter

2 tbsp (25 g) granulated sugar

For the Filling

3 (8-oz [227-g]) packages cream cheese, softened

½ cup (100 g) granulated sugar

½ cup (100 g) packed brown sugar

1 cup (240 g) canned pumpkin purée

3 large pasture-raised eggs, such as The Happy Egg Company brand or similar

1 tsp vanilla extract

1 tsp ground cinnamon

½ tsp ground nutmeg

¼ tsp ground cloves

¼ tsp salt

For the Topping

1½ cups (360 ml) sour cream

⅓ cup (67 g) granulated sugar

½ tsp vanilla extract

Preheat the oven to 350°F (175°C).

To make the crust, in a medium bowl, combine the graham cracker crumbs, butter and sugar. Give it a good stir until everything comes together. Press this crust mixture firmly into the bottom of a 9-inch (23-cm) springform pan, making sure it covers the entire bottom.

Now, let's move on to the filling. In a large mixing bowl, beat the cream cheese, granulated sugar and brown sugar until they become smooth. Add the pumpkin purée, eggs, vanilla extract, cinnamon, nutmeg, cloves and salt. Mix everything together until it's blended completely.

Pour this filling over the crust, spreading it out evenly. Place the pan on a baking sheet and pop it in the preheated oven. Bake for 55 to 60 minutes, or until the center is set and the edges are slightly golden brown.

While the cheesecake is baking, prepare the topping. In a small bowl, mix the sour cream, sugar and vanilla extract. Once the cheesecake is done baking, take it out of the oven and carefully spread the sour cream topping all over the top. Return the cheesecake to the oven for 5 minutes, allowing the topping to set. Let the cheesecake cool to room temperature in the pan. Then, let it chill in the refrigerator for at least 4 hours, or better yet overnight. When it's time to serve, carefully remove the sides of the springform pan. Cut the cake into slices and serve chilled.

LEMON RICOTTA CAKE WITH PISTACHIO CRUMBLE

Yield: 6–8 servings

The dessert flavor combination you never knew you needed is here! Introducing my Lemon Ricotta Cake with Pistachio Crumble. Get ready to indulge in a delicious lemon-infused cake, creamy ricotta cheese and a crunchy pistachio topping. This recipe takes the classic lemon cake to a whole new level with the addition of ricotta and a generous amount of pistachio crumble. It's a true crowd-pleaser, but don't just take my word for it . . . let's make it!

For the Lemon Ricotta Cake

1½ cups (180 g) all-purpose flour

1½ tsp (8 g) baking powder

½ tsp salt

½ cup (113 g) softened unsalted butter

1 cup (200 g) granulated sugar

3 large eggs

1 cup (240 g) ricotta cheese

¼ cup (60 ml) fresh lemon juice

Zest of 2 lemons

1 tsp vanilla extract

For the Pistachio Crumble

½ cup (60 g) chopped shelled pistachios

¼ cup (30 g) all-purpose flour

¼ cup (50 g) granulated sugar

2 tbsp (30 ml) melted unsalted butter

For the Lemon Glaze

1 cup (120 g) powdered sugar

2–3 tbsp (30–45 ml) fresh lemon juice

Preheat the oven to 350°F (175°C). Grease and flour a 9-inch (23-cm) round cake pan.

To make the cake, in a medium bowl, whisk together the flour, baking powder and salt. In a large mixing bowl, cream together the butter and sugar until light and fluffy. Add the eggs one at a time and continue to beat well after each addition. Mix in the ricotta cheese, lemon juice, lemon zest and vanilla extract. Gradually add the dry ingredients to the wet ingredients, mixing until just combined. Pour the batter into the cake pan and set it aside while you prepare the pistachio crumble.

To make the crumble, in a small bowl, combine the pistachios, flour, sugar and butter. Stir until the mixture resembles coarse crumbs. Sprinkle the pistachio crumble evenly over the cake batter. Bake for 35 to 40 minutes, or until a toothpick inserted into the center comes out clean.

While the cake bakes, make the lemon glaze by whisking together the powdered sugar and lemon juice in a separate bowl until smooth. Once the cake is done, let it cool in the pan for 10 minutes, and then transfer it to a wire rack to cool off completely. Then you can place the cooled cake on a serving plate and drizzle the lemon glaze over the top. Let the glaze set, about 15 minutes, before cutting the cake into slices.

BROWN BUTTER BLONDIES

Yield: 12 blondies

I believe the secret to both the perfect brownie and blondie comes from using brown butter. It adds a rich flavor that is very similar to toffee and even complements other baked goods like cookies. This recipe is my take on a blondie, using brown butter and chocolate chunks to create absolute perfection in every bite. Plus, you have the option of adding toppings like crunchy chopped nuts for extra flavor and texture. This is one of those desserts that you may want to consider making multiple batches of because these will get devoured.

1 cup (226 g) unsalted butter

2 cups (250 g) all-purpose flour

1 tsp baking powder

½ tsp salt

1½ cups (300 g) light brown sugar

2 large eggs

1 tsp vanilla extract

½ cup (90 g) chocolate chips (optional)

1 cup (150 g) chopped nuts such as walnuts or pecans (optional)

Preheat the oven to 350°F (175°C), and grease a 9 x 13-inch (23 x 33-cm) baking pan.

Place a small saucepan over medium heat. Add the unsalted butter and let it melt, stirring occasionally. Keep a close eye on it as it gradually starts to change color. Once you notice it turning golden brown and it becomes aromatic, remove the saucepan from the heat and set it aside to cool slightly.

While the brown butter cools, in a medium bowl, whisk together the flour, baking powder and salt. In a large bowl, combine the brown sugar and the brown butter. Mix them together until they are thoroughly combined and smooth. Crack the eggs into the bowl with the butter, one at a time, and mix well. Once everything is well combined, mix in the vanilla extract. Gradually add the dry mixture into the wet mixture. Stir until everything is just combined. Be careful not to overmix so you can get the best texture in the end. Then if you want, you can fold in some chocolate chips or other ingredients like walnuts or pecans for additional texture and flavor.

Pour the blondie batter into the baking pan and spread it evenly with a spatula. Bake for 25 to 30 minutes. Keep an eye on them and look for golden-brown edges and a slightly soft center. A toothpick inserted into the center should come out with a few moist crumbs to get what I consider the perfect texture. Once baked, remove the pan from the oven and let the blondies cool completely in the pan. Then, cut them into squares and get ready to enjoy the next time you need to satisfy your sweet tooth.

BOURBON CHOCOLATE PECAN PIE WITH SALTED CARAMEL DRIZZLE

Yield: 6–8 servings

One of the most incredible desserts I have ever had was at a work holiday party where all the colleagues on my team had a competition to see who could make the best treat. My boss, Eric, brought this incredible bourbon chocolate pecan pie, and I was sold. He won the contest hands-down, and instead of asking for his recipe, I really wanted to try to recreate it while also kicking it up a notch. I was able to do this through pairing the nutty, caramel and vanilla notes of bourbon with the rich, salty and complementary flavor of the salted caramel sauce for an epic treat to satisfy any sweet tooth.

For the Crust

1¼ cups (150 g) all-purpose flour

½ tsp salt

½ cup (113 g) cubed unsalted butter, cold

2–3 tbsp (30–45 ml) ice water

For the Filling

3 large eggs

1 cup (240 ml) light corn syrup

½ cup (100 g) granulated sugar

½ cup (100 g) packed brown sugar

¼ cup (60 ml) melted unsalted butter

2 tbsp (30 ml) bourbon

1 tsp vanilla extract

1 cup (120 g) chopped pecans

½ cup (90 g) semisweet chocolate chips

For the Drizzle

½ cup (100 g) granulated sugar

2 tbsp (30 ml) water

3 tbsp (45 g) unsalted butter

¼ cup (60 ml) heavy cream

¼ tsp sea salt

Preheat the oven to 350°F (175°C).

To make the pie crust, grab a food processor and combine the flour and salt. Add the butter and pulse until the mixture resembles coarse crumbs. Gradually add the ice water, 1 tablespoon (15 ml) at a time, and pulse until the dough comes together and forms a ball. Be careful not to overdo it by adding too much water. Transfer the dough to a floured surface and shape it into a flat disk. Wrap it in plastic wrap and refrigerate for at least 30 minutes to relax. Once the dough has chilled, roll it out onto a floured surface. It should be large enough to fit a 9-inch (23-cm) pie dish. Transfer the dough to the dish, trim any excess off the top and crimp down the edges if you prefer.

To make the filling, in a large bowl, whisk together the eggs, corn syrup, granulated sugar, brown sugar, melted butter, bourbon and vanilla extract until smooth. Stir in the pecans and chocolate chips, making sure they are spread throughout.

Pour the filling into the prepared pie crust, spreading it evenly. Place the pie on a baking sheet to catch any drips and bake for 45 to 55 minutes. Keep an eye on it—when the center is set and the crust turns golden brown, your pie is ready.

While the pie bakes, make the salted caramel drizzle. In a small saucepan, add the sugar and water and cook over medium heat, swirling the pan occasionally. When the sugar dissolves and turns a beautiful amber color, carefully whisk in the butter until it's smooth and well combined. Now we can remove the saucepan from the heat and carefully whisk in the heavy cream. The mixture will bubble up, so be careful here. Stir in the sea salt until well incorporated, and let the caramel cool slightly, allowing it to thicken. Once the pie is done, let it cool on a wire rack. Then you can finish it off with a drizzle of the caramel, and you are ready to wow everyone.

CHAI SPICED RICE PUDDING

Yield: 4-6 servings

The aroma coming from anything chai spiced is so comforting, and it makes it one of my favorite things to indulge in. I love the idea of using these flavors more, and I decided to incorporate the fragrant spices from chai into a creamy and sweet rice pudding. You can garnish with chopped nuts or dried fruits and really find the best flavor combination for you.

1 cup (200 g) uncooked basmati rice

4 cups (960 ml) whole milk

½ cup (100 g) granulated sugar

1 cinnamon stick

4 green cardamom pods, lightly crushed

4 whole cloves

¼ tsp ground ginger

¼ tsp ground cinnamon, plus more for dusting

¼ tsp ground nutmeg

¼ tsp ground cardamom

¼ tsp vanilla extract

½ cup (80 g) raisins or chopped dried apricots (optional)

Chopped nuts such as almonds, pistachios or cashews, for garnishing

Rinse the basmati rice under cold water until the water runs clear. Drain the rice and set it aside.

In a large saucepan, combine the milk, sugar, cinnamon stick, cardamom pods, cloves, ginger, cinnamon, nutmeg and cardamom, and bring the mixture to a simmer over medium heat. Stir occasionally, and once it's at a steady simmer, add the rice to the saucepan and give it a stir. Reduce the heat to low and let the rice cook in the milk mixture, and keep stirring occasionally for 30 to 35 minutes.

Once the rice is cooked and the mixture is creamy and thickened, remove the pan from the heat and remove and discard the cinnamon stick, cardamom pods and cloves. Stir in the vanilla extract and raisins (if using) and transfer the pudding to serving bowls or glasses. Allow it to cool slightly, then cover and refrigerate for at least 2 hours, or until it is chilled and set.

Before serving, top the pudding with chopped nuts, and finish it off with a dusting of cinnamon. Serve chilled and enjoy that perfectly creamy texture and amazing chai spices.

BOOZY PECAN BOURBON BALLS

Yield: 5-6 servings

I remember the first time someone made these pecan bourbon balls for me. I was immediately hooked. They absolutely pack a punch and can be very bourbon forward, but I will never complain about that. Not only do they taste amazing, but they are also so easy to make and require no oven or special tools. These make a great gift, treat and guilty pleasure for anyone who is a fan of bourbon.

1½ cups (180 g) finely chopped pecans

1 cup (100 g) vanilla wafer crumbs

1 cup (120 g) powdered sugar, divided

¼ cup (25 g) + 2 tbsp (10 g) unsweetened cocoa powder, divided

¼ cup (60 ml) bourbon whiskey

2 tbsp (30 ml) light corn syrup

½ tsp vanilla extract

In a large bowl, combine the pecans, vanilla wafer crumbs, ½ cup (60 g) of the powdered sugar and 2 tablespoons (10 g) of the cocoa powder. Mix everything together and set aside. In a small bowl, mix together the bourbon, corn syrup and vanilla extract. Pour the mixture over the pecan mixture and stir until well combined. The mixture should hold together when pressed. Feel free to use your hands to achieve the best consistency. Cover the bowl with plastic wrap and refrigerate for at least 1 hour. This chilling time will firm up the mixture, making it easier to shape into the balls.

When it's nice and chilled, shape the chilled pecan mixture into 1-inch (2.5-cm)-diameter balls. Add the remaining sugar in a shallow bowl. Add the remaining cocoa powder in a separate shallow bowl. Roll each ball in either powdered sugar or cocoa powder until they are all evenly coated. You can alternate between the two coatings to create a variety of flavors and appearances. Then place the coated bourbon balls on a baking sheet lined with parchment paper. Repeat the process until all the balls are coated and arranged neatly on the baking sheet. Refrigerate the balls for at least 1 hour to allow them to firm up, and then they are ready to enjoy.

LONDON FOG CRÈME BRÛLÉE

Yield: 6 servings

It's hard to beat a London fog latte on a brisk and chilly day. The way the herbal flavors complement each other is perfect, and when made right, it's easily one of my favorite drinks. I wanted to find a way to bring what I love about the taste of a London fog to a dessert, and what better vessel than a crème brûlée. This is a dessert that you can make ahead of time and surprise everyone with—an incredible treat paired with the satisfying crunch and texture of a crème brûlée.

2 cups (480 ml) heavy cream

½ cup (120 ml) whole milk

¼ cup (50 g) granulated sugar, plus more for caramelizing

4 Earl Grey tea bags

6 large egg yolks

1 tsp vanilla extract

Preheat the oven to 325°F (163°C), and place six ramekins or custard cups in a baking dish.

In a saucepan, add the cream, milk and sugar. Heat this mixture until it simmers while stirring it occasionally. Remove the saucepan from the heat, and add the tea bags. Let them steep for 10 to 12 minutes to infuse the cream with their delightful flavors. Then, discard the tea bags.

In a medium bowl, whisk the egg yolks and vanilla extract until smooth and creamy. Slowly pour the hot mixture into the beaten egg yolks while whisking continuously. Then strain the mixture through a sieve to get the best texture.

Divide the custard mixture among the prepared ramekins. Place the baking dish with the ramekins in a larger pan filled with hot water, surrounding them in a water bath. Bake the custards for 40 to 45 minutes, or until the edges are set but the center has a slight jiggle. Remove the ramekins from the water bath and let them cool on a wire rack. After that, refrigerate for at least 2 hours to let them set.

Just before serving, sprinkle a layer of granulated sugar over the custard. Caramelize the sugar using a kitchen torch until golden brown, creating a crunchy crust that everyone loves to break as much as they do to eat.

CAFÉ MOCHA MOUSSE WITH ORANGE MOUSSE LAYERS

Yield: 3-4 servings

Prepare to indulge in this heavenly combination! This delightful dessert brings together the rich flavors of chocolate and coffee in the café mocha mousse, while the orange mousse adds a refreshing citrusy twist. Each layer is light, creamy and utterly irresistible. Let's jump right into the recipe and create this decadent treat.

For Café Mocha Mousse

1 cup (240 ml) heavy cream

2 tbsp (15 g) powdered sugar

2 tbsp (10 g) unsweetened cocoa powder

1 tsp instant coffee granules

4 oz (113 g) semisweet chocolate, chopped

2 large egg yolks

1 tsp vanilla extract

For Orange Mousse

1 cup (240 ml) heavy cream

2 tbsp (15 g) powdered sugar

4 oz (113 g) white chocolate, chopped

2 large egg yolks

1 tsp orange zest

2 tbsp (30 ml) freshly squeezed orange juice

1 tsp vanilla extract

Whipped cream (optional)

Cacao nibs (optional)

To make the café mocha mousse, in a medium bowl, add the cream and powdered sugar, and beat until soft peaks form. Set aside. In a small bowl, combine the cocoa powder and coffee granules and set aside.

Create a double boiler system by placing a heatproof bowl over a pot of simmering water. Melt the semisweet chocolate in the bowl, stirring until it's smooth. Remove it from the heat and let it cool slightly.

In another bowl, whisk together the egg yolks and vanilla extract until smooth and well combined. Gradually pour the melted chocolate into the egg yolk mixture, whisking until well combined. Add the cocoa-coffee mixture to the chocolate mixture and whisk until smooth. Gently fold the whipped cream into the chocolate mixture until well incorporated. Divide evenly into serving glasses or bowls, and refrigerate for at least 2 hours to allow it to set.

Now we can make the Orange Mousse. In a medium bowl, add the cream and powdered sugar, and beat until soft peaks form. Set aside.

Create a double boiler system once more and melt the white chocolate, stirring occasionally until smooth. Remove it from the heat and let it cool slightly.

In another bowl, whisk together the egg yolks, orange zest, orange juice and vanilla extract until smooth and well combined. Gradually pour the melted white chocolate into the egg yolk mixture, whisking until well combined. Gently fold the whipped cream into the mixture and divide evenly on top of the set café mocha mousse. Refrigerate for 2 hours or until fully set. These layers of flavor work perfectly with each other and taste absolutely amazing. Feel free to top it off with some whipped cream and whatever else you like. I prefer to use cacao nibs; they work so well with the flavors in this dessert.

ACKNOWLEDGMENTS

I want to start off by thanking my family for all the support and motivation in everything I do. My girlfriend, Amber, lets me convert the kitchen into a studio almost daily, while also turning our home bar into storage for all my cooking and filming equipment. Both she and our son, Bryson, double as my taste-testers and critics, and without them, this book would not have been possible. I love you both more than words can describe.

To my sister, Hunter, and brother-in-law, Corey, for being a big part of the process and being so flexible. Corey and I worked weekly on photoshoots for the cookbook, and I couldn't be prouder of having such an incredible talent in the family who I get to share this opportunity with. Not only did this experience create precious memories for all, but it also gave my son and niece, Blake, more time together to create an amazing bond that makes us all a very happy. I love you all.

To my mom, Kim, and my twin sister, Amanda, for always being there throughout the years in support of any new adventure I took on. You all were and are the support system that got me through my early years, and still help so much to this day. Mom showed me what a true work ethic looked like, and without her as a role model, I have no idea where I would be. Amanda and I had competitions every step of the way, and her drive to succeed and work hard has always been inspiring. I love you both.

To my late Papa Bernie, who taught me what being a man of your word really means. The man who was there for me as a role model, father figure and cheerleader up until the day he passed. You were the best man I have ever known, and I wish I could share these incredible recipes with you. I love and miss you very much.

To my incredible community that supports all that I do under Alf's Kitchen. I wouldn't be writing this book without your support, and I hope every single one of you knows that you are a big part of this process, and I appreciate everything so much. The comments, video shares, messages and love shared over the past two years mean the world to me.

To the team at Page Street Publishing, thank you so much for the guidance and understanding that I needed as a new author. With your support and this opportunity, we put together a piece of work I couldn't be more proud of.

To my team over at Viral Nation, thank you for being there for support and advice, and for looking out for me in my business endeavors. The world of an online content creator can get insane at times, and your support is appreciated on so many levels.

To the team at Dalstrong, especially Abby, for being an early believer in me and my content, and always keeping me stocked with some of the best cookware and knives in the business. The partnership that we built early on is something I will never forget. Thank you for believing in me.

To the team at Meat N' Bone, thank you for all your support. Creating content to post almost daily can get really pricey, and I loved your products long before we started working together. Gabriel and the team are such an asset to me, and I am honored to work together to spread a great message.

ABOUT THE AUTHOR

Mike Alfarah is the lifelong foodie and self-taught home chef behind @alfskitchen_. He started cooking more than 20 years ago and developed a passion for flavor that now translates to millions of views each month across his social media. He believes in thinking outside of the box when it comes to food and loves helping others get comfortable with trying new things in the kitchen. He has an amazing community of fellow creators, chefs, supporters and foodies that all come together to enjoy food with a fun twist. Mike has also worked with some incredible brands over the years, including Dalstrong, Whole Foods, Ninja, Lodge Cast Iron and Cuso Cuts™ to name a few.

When Mike is not in the kitchen or working on creating content, he is spending time with family and friends on the golf course, taking a day trip with his girlfriend and son or helping businesses in his community as a full-time business banker and social media consultant. He is always looking for his next adventure.

Mike lives in Northwest Ohio with his girlfriend, Amber, and son, Bryson.

INDEX